dsW
march 1957

# FOUR CENTURIES OF
## FINE PRINTING

# FOUR CENTURIES OF
# FINE PRINTING

*Two Hundred and Seventy-two Examples*
*of the Work of Presses established*
*between 1465 and 1924*

*With an Introduction*

BY

STANLEY MORISON

LONDON
ERNEST BENN LIMITED

FIRST PUBLISHED IN A LIMITED FOLIO
EDITION OF 400 COPIES, 1924
SECOND (REVISED, OCTAVO) EDITION, 1949

MADE IN GREAT BRITAIN
PUBLISHED BY ERNEST BENN LIMITED
BOUVERIE HOUSE, FLEET STREET, LONDON, E.C.4
AND PRINTED BY R. & R. CLARK LTD., EDINBURGH

# PREFACE

THIS is a volume of reproductions of pages and title-pages from books composed in the "roman" form of letter immediately related to that used by printers today for books, newspapers, catalogues, etc. The first roman was cut for two printers at Subiaco, near Rome, for a text of Cicero's *De Oratore* in 1465, and it is the first plate in the book. Printing of the fifteenth century has already been so considerably studied and is so amply illustrated elsewhere that the exhibits from this period are reduced to a minimum. Hence the bulk of the volume is devoted to the work of the four later centuries. The earlier pieces given will, I hope, be sufficient to introduce the reader to the work of the first Italian printers.

The specimens are grouped, as a rule, in order of time and place. Where possible the inclusion of specimens with which the reader may have become familiarised by illustration elsewhere has been avoided. In most instances the title-page best displays the book's typographical character and presents a representative exhibit of the style and skill of the individual printer. In numerous instances additional examples are shown, *e.g.* a number of pages are taken from the pretty 12mo *Calendier Historial* (Jean de Tournes, Lyons, 1563) and from the splendid folio *Livre de Perspective* of Jean Cousin (Paris, 1560).

The illustrations are selected, in the main, from books of general interest rather than musical, legal, liturgical and biblical texts. The pages from the *Horae* of Geofroy Tory, or the *Bible*

5

and *New Testament* of Jean de Tournes, are shown for the interest of their decoration. In every case the type area of the original page is indicated, as most of the specimens are necessarily printed in reduced size in this octavo edition.

It is a pleasant duty to record my obligations to the officials of the British Museum, above all to Mr. A. F. Johnson; to MM. Châtelain and Beaulieux of the Library of the Sorbonne; Dr. Guido Biagi of the Laurenziana, Florence; to Mr. George Parker Winship of the Widener Library, Cambridge, U.S.A.; to the late Berkeley Updike of the Merrymount Press, Boston, U.S.A., and to Mr. Bruce Rogers, for kindly lending me specimens of their work; to the late A. W. Evans, Messrs. H. V. Marrot, A. Ehrman, A. Zwemmer and Ernest Maggs, for lending me scarce volumes from their collections; and to Mr. Conan Nicholas for assistance with the proofs and index.

My greatest debt, however, is to the admirably arranged Grisebach collection in the Library of the Berlin Kunstgewerbe Museum, to which, by the kindness of the Keeper, Dr. Peter Jessen, I was enabled to refer freely and informally at a time, soon after the end of the 1914–18 War, when visitors from Britain were few. From 1921 Dr. Jessen was good enough, by correspondence, to help my typographical studies that were then just beginning.

This book was my first published contribution to the study of printing. The original edition of 1924 was limited to 400 copies for Great Britain. The format measured 13 by 18 inches, comprising upwards of six hundred examples reproduced in collotype. A German edition was printed under the title *Meisterdrucke aus vier Jahrhunderten* and a French edition under the title *Les plus belles pages de l'imprimerie*. Some of the illustrations were later reproduced by the half-tone process in a volume which the present publishers entitled *The Art of the Printer*.

In the present demy octavo edition, only a few revisions in the text have been made. Some new examples have been added to the plates, of which nearly three hundred are included. The book is reprinted, after twenty-five years, on the initiative of the publishers of the original edition, and I desire to thank them for making it available to a wider public on both sides of the Atlantic.

S. M.

London
*September* 1948

# CONTENTS

9

# FOUR CENTURIES OF FINE PRINTING

## I

As a definition I suggest that for the present purpose "printing" shall be the device of placing together moveable pieces of metal (types) each having upon its upper end a character in relief, which, being inked and impressed upon suitable material, leaves a mark, or "print".

The designing of the letters and their founding upon metal bodies precede the several processes involved in their composition into words, building into pages, inking and impressing upon the selected material. When all has been accomplished with ordinary care there will issue that very useful production, a piece of clear printing.

Printing can be much more than this. When all these processes are conducted by a man of exceptional talent and skill the result of his work will be an exceptional piece of printing. The *fine* printer begins where the careful printer has left off. For "fine" printing something is required in addition to care—certain vital gifts of the mind and understanding. Only when these are added to a knowledge of the technical processes will there result a piece of design, *i.e.* a work expressing logic, consistency and personality. Fine printing may be described as the product of a lively and seasoned intelligence working with carefully chosen type, ink and paper. Of all the printer's materials, that which contributes most immediately to the fineness or otherwise of the product is his type. Though a competent designer may, by the agreeable disposition of his lines, go far towards redeeming the page from the original sin of bad letter, the work, whatever his cunning, will never be above criticism. The necessity of fine letter to fine printing is, however, too plain to need justification here. It is otherwise with the principles of selection of fine letter: these are less obvious. Apart from that will-o'-the-wisp "legibility", what light can be thrown on the question: in what does fine letter, the necessary preliminary to fine printing, consist?

First it must be borne in mind that a fine book is more than "something to read". The amateur looks for character in printing. The book, therefore, which essays to rank above the commonplace, will, while not failing in its essential purpose, carry the personality of its maker no less surely than that of its author and its subject. The problem of the typographer is to achieve an individual book without doing violence to its essential purpose, or to any accidental character conferred by an artist or book-decorator. Thus the whole mystery of fine typography lies in the perfect reconciliation of these interests. Moreover, there is here no master-formula: almost every book is a challenge to the artist-typographer.

The practice of varying the type with the nature of the text goes farther back than the age of its invention, and there can be no doubt that in our own day the vast increase, not only of printing but of kinds of printing, requires the use of different kinds of type. In the early history of the craft the conservatism of the clerical and legal professions long secured the retention of gothic types for liturgical and legal texts. The letter which we call "roman" was then largely restricted to classical texts, but is today in universal use even by ecclesiastics and lawyers. There is, in consequence, little opportunity for the use of black letter. This, as I think, unfortunate result makes us even less patient of the notion that there is, or may be, a best of all types of universal application and appropriateness. Satisfaction indeed comes no more easily to the typographical than to any other enthusiast. Whether of today or yesterday, the fine printer in his zeal is continually adding here and modifying there. In his wisdom he changes his type-form but little; for, as the reading public is multiplied to a figure beyond the imagination of any Aldus or Plantin, the alphabetical code must of necessity remain stable. The bizarre evolutions of the German calligrapher between the wars are the experiments of those to whom the roman letter is still a relative novelty. In much of its finest work the rest of the world is going back for its models to the day when the roman letter was a novelty to all save the Romans.

Here indeed the typographer and the calligrapher find their first *datum*: that set of capitals evolved by the epigraphers of first-century Rome. These are the master patterns which must rule our alphabets. This is not to say that the only satisfactory capitals are those which exactly reproduce these classical forms or which are built according to the geometrical formulae elaborated by Luca de Pacioli in 1509, or the copies made by Dürer in 1525 and Tory in 1529. These mechanical devices afford an admirable exercise—and no more. The fine letter must be as free from the mechanical perfection of set-square and compass as from the monotony of laboured characterisation. It must be understood then, that by requiring types to be built according to the essential form of classical roman inscribed letters, we do not by the same rule exclude either the individuality of the craftsman or the felicity of the tool he uses, but only the tendency towards corruption and complication of originally pure and simple lines.

What the craftsman of trained eye and hand can do with the classical roman shape may be seen from the lettering round the finest portrait medals of the renaissance. I need do no more than cite such a finished example as Pisanello's "Malatesta" and "Lysippus Junior's" portrait medal of himself. A comparison will reveal the fact that whereas the essential form is the same, the characterisation is very different. The difference is to be found in the craftsman and his tool. *Tot homines.* . . . There need therefore be no fear that with the classical capitals as a basis we are keeping the art of letter design in a strait waist-coat. Thus, in a word, it is for the typographer to meditate upon the ancient forms, to digest them, to make them his own and then to draw. He will find that it requires consummate sensitiveness and skill, first to form the letters and, secondly, so to set them upon type bodies that none is conspicuous in weight and that each sorts with the greatest fellowship of feeling and colour with the small letters. These small letters, lower-case as printers call them (or in the language of palaeographers, *minuscules*), represent an even more difficult problem.

Here we have a set of models possessing nothing like the authority and finality of the simple classic roman capitals. We have inherited instead a series of mixed forms, some extending above and others below the normal lines; some of these are simple rigid letters like v w x z immediately derived from the capitals, and others are more complex and curved forms like g q, etc., which afford a maximum of opportunity for modification, variation and corruption. Is there an essential form of these letters? By what authority may we impose it? A little history may tell us.

Lower-case letters developed during the sixth to the eighth century, through the uncial and half-uncial stages. Independence was secured in the eighth century, when the so-called caroline minuscule (still essentially roman in derivation) was developed. It is this type of writing mediated to us by scribes of the fifteenth century which is the model for our lower-case letters. The caroline minuscule when wrought to perfection was a magnificent letter; it was clear, symmetrical and, above all, simple. Nevertheless succeeding centuries witnessed the engrafting upon it of a very important and far-reaching modification, *i.e.* a gradual movement from the original, round and open, into a pointed and condensed character. This is our so-called "gothic".

The gothic script plainly represents not so much a departure from, as a variation of, the caroline letter. It is often of the greatest beauty; and it may be contended with some show of reason that, by transforming curves into joints, the gothic writers secured for their alphabet a greater degree of homogeneity than resides either in the caroline or in the neo-caroline letter to which we as printers are immediately indebted for our present-day types.

With the fifteenth century there came an intensely deliberate reversion to an aesthetic based in an enthusiasm for the civilisation and culture of ancient Rome. The eyes of all, including calligraphers, became fascinated by pre-gothic art and literature. Thus it happened that, for the transcription of classical texts, the scribes under the direction of artists and scholars turned aside from their inherited black letter and founded a new hand upon the basis of that in which their classical originals were most frequently preserved. Since known as neo-caroline, the new hand was anything but a reproduction even of the ninth-century minuscule. Perhaps, however, the experiment is most noteworthy in respect to its treatment of the majuscules. A whole-hearted reversion to the ancient stone letters marked the capitals of the new script in its mature form.

This early renaissance hand, though founded upon the caroline minuscule, is significantly different from its predecessors. Its minuscule is slightly compressed, though very much rounder than the pointed gothic which it supplanted; its perpendiculars are well proportioned, and over all there is a note of the characteristic elegance which was so diligently sought by the scribes of the time. They were immediately concerned to rival the beauty of all existing manuscripts; and in spite of the appeal of fine codices in the half-uncial and caroline scripts, there can be little doubt that their ambition was realised. It may be argued, and I think successfully, that the finest gothic MSS. of the thirteenth century are uniquely beautiful, that the gothic letter in its best form possesses a picturesqueness, a vigour, versatility and a dramatic quality not surpassed by the pure roman letter. Nevertheless the greater simplicity and elasticity of the pure roman letter predestined for it a much wider use. Nor is the renaissance hand merely practical. Even in its earliest form it is exceedingly beautiful.

Among the earliest MSS. in this letter is a Valerius Flaccus written in Florence by one Antonio di Mario, who completed it—according to the colophon on his last page—in December of the year 1429 (MS. Laur. 39, 35, cf. Vitelli e Paoli, *Collezione florentina di facsimili paleografici*, Firenze, 1886, serie latini, tav. 48). In this MS. the majuscules retain certain gothic characteristics though the minuscules are well formed. The new letter was not perfected for a decade or two. The exact year of the foundation at Florence of Niccolò de' Niccoli's school of calligraphy is apparently not known; but the famous humanist died in 1447, and it is suggested by the Neapolitan scholar Nicola Barone that the MS. to which we have referred is the outcome of his foundation. This would mean that the school was founded *circa* 1425. However it may have been, it is certain that there were other humanists beside Niccoli, men like Poggio for example, who founded schools for teaching the new hand, and that Florence was the centre of a movement which spread rapidly. The seventeenth general council, which debated for nine months the relations of the eastern and western Churches, was held at Florence, 1439; and it is likely enough that on this occasion the advantages of the new script were noticed by the secretaries and notaries who came in the train of hundreds of bishops of the west. Certain it is that the new hand soon conquered Rome. It was accepted by Nicholas V in 1447 for use in the Vatican chancery as the distinctive hand for the engrossing of papal briefs—but with a difference. The roman practice was to slope the minuscules while retaining upright majuscules.

## II

And this brings us to the thorny subject of nomenclature, involving definition where none exists. So far in this discussion I have ventured to allude to the renaissance hand as a pure roman hand. It is known to Italian palaeographers as the *scrittura umanistica* (so Barone, Carta, Vitelli, Biagi), to the French as *écriture de la renaissance* (de Wailly, Giry), and to the Germans *humanistische Schrift* (Steffens). In the opinion of English palaeographers "humanistic" is a thoroughly unscientific term. They find it preferable to use *roman* just as the printer does. But the term "roman" will sound well only to those who think of gothic, beneventan or other national hands as essentially "non-roman". The difficulty increases with the development of the sloping form of the same minuscule. It has always been the English custom to distinguish upright and inclined letters of this renaissance kind, whether in MS. or in print, by the terms roman and italic respectively, in spite of the obvious fact that the so-called roman is most probably florentine, and the so-called italic perhaps roman. We have accustomed ourselves to regard italic as essentially a sloped letter. It will be found, I think, that in this matter of terminology, whether calligraphical or typographical, the Germans have the best of it; for our "roman", their equivalent is "antiqua", for italic, "kursiv". The term "antiqua" is not without excellent precedents. A very fine Athanasius exists in the Biblioteca Nazionale at Turin. It was written in an upright hand at Naples in 1492–93 by Ioannes Rainaldus Mennius for Ferdinand of Aragon. When Professor Nicola Barone was working in the Neapolitan archives he came across a receipt signed by the calligrapher: "Giovanni Rinaldo Mennio ... riceve 6 duc. per la scrittura in lettera antica di 4 quinterni dell' opera de Atanasio" (so N. Barone, *Cedole di tesoreria dell' archivi di stato di Napoli*, 148/678). Other similar

B

terms may be found in contemporary use, *lettera antica nuova*, *lettera rotonda*, and, applied to capitals only, *lettera romana*, *lettere romane antiche*. On the other hand the more running, ligatured and less formal script used in diplomatic documents and in correspondence was known as *cancellerescha* (which is little use when we recollect the running gothic script of the eleventh to the fourteenth centuries current under the same name), and also *corsiva*. Nearly always the *corsiva* was slightly inclined. Cursive hands are, however, found in which the letters are upright, or mostly upright. In nearly every instance the capitals are upright. We are accustomed to think of cursive, or italic, as essentially a sloped letter, whereas there remain specimens of this type in which all the current characteristics of the cursive script exist, except that neither the capital nor the lower-case is sloped. It will be seen, therefore, that a scientific terminology to cover the roman letter in its fourteenth-, fifteenth- and sixteenth-century variations is overdue. That the matter is an important one and not of mere specialist interest will be appreciated when it is desired to make a classification of types. Fortunately it is not necessary to do this in any considerable detail, since the present volume does not attempt a complete history of the roman letter, but rather an exhibition of the growth of typographical style.

Since a one-volume treatment of the subject must accept severe limitations, I have sought to exemplify the development of the typography which employs that union of the ancient roman capitals with the mid-fifteenth-century lower-case, which we call "roman type". The examples begin with a page from Cicero's *De Oratore* printed by Schweynheym and Pannartz at Subiaco in 1465. The type appears to agree with a scientific definition of the word "roman", and would have been recognised by contemporary calligraphers as an adequate reproduction of the hand they knew and practised as humanistic. The two Germans, removing from Subiaco, set up a press in Rome in the palace of the De' Massimi family. Here they printed a Cicero (1467) in a roughly cast roman letter of little grace, compared with which the Da Spira type (1470) clearly represents a vast improvement; but not an absolute invention as was boldly claimed by the brothers.

A rather more mellow appearance attaches to the work of Nicolas Jenson, produced from 1470; but it does not materially differ from that of the Da Spiras—it would seem that their example was far from lost upon Jenson. The latter's editions, however, quickly achieved a higher reputation than was secured by any other printer. Jenson's associate and successor, Herbort, issued a catalogue of books for sale (? 1482) which, after the manner of advertisers, contained a lengthy commendation of Jenson's types wherein exaggeration was certainly not lacking. After speaking of the correctness of the Jenson editions he proceeds to claim that "the quality and value of his types is another marvel to relate for it ought to be ascribed rather to divine inspiration than human wit". The panegyrist is, however, well within the mark when he claims that "the characters are so methodically and carefully finished by that famous man that the letters are not smaller or larger or thicker than reason demands or than may afford pleasure".

In spite of Jenson's almost divinely assisted craftsmanship, fine writing nevertheless was elsewhere so highly esteemed that even his printing failed to please many contemporary collectors of books. The bibliophiles of Florence insisted that it was so inferior to the manuscript as to be unworthy of their libraries. It may be well to point out here that whatever preferences some of us may have for the illuminations and miniatures of an earlier age, it can well be claimed that calligraphy was at its best during the hundred and twenty years after the foundation of the writing schools in Florence by Niccolò de' Niccoli, Poggio Bracciolini and others. The productions of these schools were at their finest just at the time when there were issuing from the Venetian press the books of Jenson which modern amateurs

are prone to rank as the finest achievement of all time. Their
excellence almost persuades one authority to doubt that they
were made with human hands. Notwithstanding, it may be
judged that the Florentine *conoscenti* were right in their pre-
ference for the work of Antonio Sinibaldi, Pietro Strozzi and
Gherardo di Giovanni del Ciriago and other scribes, whose
work was utilised by Lorenzo the Magnificent, Federigo duke
of Urbino, and by Ferdinand of Aragon, who even put himself
to the pains of bringing Sinibaldi and Strozzi to Naples.

Quite apart from the matter of decoration which all printers
before, and many after Erhard Ratdolt, left to professional
designers outside the office, it is certain that Jenson's letters are
individually less satisfactory than those of Sinibaldi; nor is this
surprising. Twelve years before Nicolas Jenson settled at Venice
as typefounder and printer he was mint-master at Tours. In the
exercise of this craft such lettering as he needed to engrave would
almost exclusively have been capitals, just as the founder of the
medallic art, Pisanello, never employed lower-case. But with
Sinibaldi the conditions were very different; his eye and pen
were practised in the formation of fine lower-case and in the
achievement of the greatest possible ease in combination of
capitals and small letters. In any case, the elasticity and freedom
of his pen gave it tremendous advantages in combining power
over that of the metal punch and type body; and in addition it
was an essential point of the Florentine calligraphic school to
follow a manuscript tradition which had existed at least since
the caroline reform of the ninth century. Sinibaldi and his
peers, unlike Jenson, made their upper-case noticeably shorter
than the ascending lower-case letters b d f l, etc., and by this
means prevented their capitals from becoming conspicuous
when combined with the small letters. Jenson elevated his
capitals almost to the height of these ascending letters and
thereby gave his printed page a certain spottiness; that is to
say, the eye is attracted to the masses of form and colour

representing the capitals. In homogeneity, therefore, the finest
Florentine manuscript is superior to the printed book of Jenson,
as it must inevitably be in respect of elasticity, sharpness, decoration and, above all, of personality.

In the light of the welcome that printing received at Venice
we cannot but be surprised at the coldness shown to it at
Florence. In so mean an estimate was typography held in the
city of Cimabue, Giotto and Michelangelo that its first book
was issued almost two years after the publication of Jenson's
Eusebius; and, much more to our astonishment, only six years
before the introduction of printing into London. Nor is the
first Florentine printing of anything but the slightest interest.
It was a Virgil printed by Cennini, a capable goldsmith enough,
but who, unlike the Venetians, lacked the patronage of the
artists and nobles of his city; yet he worked at a time of
unparalleled enthusiasm for scholarship and for letters. The
celebrated Medici Library, begun in 1444 by Cosimo, and
opened by him to all scholars, contained thousands of Greek and
Latin books. Federigo Montefeltro, duke of Urbino, was another
enthusiast who by means of his ample resources strove to
emulate Cosimo's example. That great bookseller of Florence,
Vespasiano da Bisticci, *princeps librariorum florentinorum*, played
a great part in assembling the collections of the Medici and of
the Aragonese Court at Naples. His *Vite di uomini illustri del
secolo XV* describes at length the library made by the duke with
his help, and he adds the words: "In this library all the books
are superlatively good, all are written with the pen; and were
there a single printed book it would have been ashamed in
such company. All are most beautifully illuminated and
written on vellum."

It cannot be doubted that these words were written with
great deliberation and feeling. Vespasiano was himself a master
scribe and at that time the largest employer of copyists in all
Italy. Printing would need to be fine to satisfy the taste of such

a man, and though we may well admit in parenthesis that Vespasiano's vested interests as well as his sympathies lay in the scriptoria, it is demonstrable that his judgement was sincere. At least he could hardly have been expected to be a friend to such poor printing as Cennini produced. In this connection it may be recalled that, according to the estimate of their latest biographer, the Medici family alone spent upon books a sum equal in present money to some three millions sterling. An immense sum therefore passed through the hands of Vespasiano to the Florentine scribes, illuminators and miniaturists. Venice—in spite of its maritime trade and wealthy syndics, at this time on the decline—never knew such spendthrift enthusiasts as the Medici.

Lorenzo, however, was induced to patronise printing, and actually accepted the dedication of several volumes issued by the Giuntas of his city. But nothing better illustrates the temperamental difference between Florence and Venice in their attitude to printing than the fact that as many as 4000 or more books or editions were produced in the latter city during the fifteenth century. The typography of Venice thus reflects both the high accomplishment of its artists and the progressive instinct of an essentially vigorous maritime city. The Florentine school, on the other hand, while going beyond the excellence of the Venetian school in painting and knowing no rival in sculpture, pursued the arts of miniature-painting and of calligraphy with a conservatism in which printing could find little or no place. We cannot doubt that masterpieces greater than Venice ever gave us awaited the collaboration of Sinibaldi the scribe and Gherico the miniaturist with a craftsman-printer of Jenson's calibre; but by the time of the death of Lorenzo the Magnificent, Florentine printing was hardly out of its cradle, and except for experiments in illustration, offers scant typographical interest before the time of Lorenzo Torrentino (1547).

Thus the mightiest intellectual and artistic centre of modern times, surpassed in conservatism only by Rome itself, almost refused to admit the printing press. The consequences were notable. The irresistible practical advantages of the invention were welcomed by a city which, if it lacked in some degree the cultivation and the artistic competence of its neighbouring city, enjoyed the compensation of greater practicality and clearer vision.

Venice naturally gained by its position on the great highway between Germany and Italy over the Brenner Pass, and thus, being one of the first important places which German crafts-men would meet on their way south, it assumed a position in the art of typography which quickly grew to be paramount. The mere invention in 1469 by Johann van Speier (da Spira) of what is now recognised to be a really fine roman letter con-ferred upon the city a distinction which his successors more than maintained. It remains a matter for keen regret that the manuscript tradition of subordinating the majuscules in the interest of homogeneity was not followed in the city of Venice, whose typographical authority became, with the ad-vent of Jenson, nothing less than magisterial. The renowned Frenchman's books, even though their pages are marred by heavy capitals, are technically fine, business-like volumes. They secured such a reputation that though many have criticised his press-work none has ventured to criticise either his composition or the design of his type. His setting is careful, he leaves no ugly white at the end of his sentences, and if his books were often spoiled by hand decoration it was not of the master's applica-tion. Jenson's services to typography are undoubtedly unique, but it may be perhaps that his work has been honoured more by superstitious adoration than by discerning worship. His books are not novelties, and herein lay Jenson's strength: he worked carefully within the limits of a fine if rigid convention. It is important to note this in appraising early printing.

## III

The tradition, or at least the memory, of fine writing which the local scribes bequeathed to the printers who ousted them, protected the fifteenth-century printed book from the introduction of novelties, experiments and eccentricities. The printer's necessity was to make his book as much as possible like the scribe's. The writers communicated to their successors not only the craft of drawing letters but the equally high mystery of handsomely placing the matter upon the page—or we should rather say, *pair* of pages, since it is impossible to open any text without envisaging the pair. Much of the grandeur of early books is due to the generosity of their margins, and it may be that present-day amateurs have more to learn from the *mise en page* of Jenson than from anything else of his. The press-work of these books is often as bad as good. In this matter Ratdolt is considerably Jenson's superior, but both appreciated the fact that as they had chosen to work in roman letter so they were bound to leave aside the gothic and its ideal, the black page. The rounder, slighter, roman letter means not a black but a grey page. The roman means indeed a totally different sort of book, slenderer type, therefore greyer page, thinner paper, and slighter binding. In a word, the roman book is a typical renaissance product, just as the black letter is gothic. The lightness of line in the roman character naturally induced a correspondingly fine line in book illustration. The grey page therefore (and it is worth repeating) is the renaissance product just as the black page is the mediaeval. And here it may be observed that the wood-cutters who supplied the decorations and illustrations to early Italian books were not necessarily the artists of the designs but merely the artificers. They were competent craftsmen, making it their business to effect the greatest harmony between the printer's type and their cut. If in many cases it may be felt that their title devices and illustrations tend to be so large as to be more successful as single sheets, there can be no two opinions about the *Poliphilus* (1499) of Aldus Manutius. Here indeed the wood-engravers produced a masterpiece. In spite of the excellence of Francesco Griffo's roman letter the volume owes its reputation entirely to its cuts. Nevertheless this fine type, and even more its first state used in Pietro Bembo's dialogue *De Aetna*, printed by Aldus in 1495, justifies a paragraph as well as a picture. The type is indeed a notable one. It is clear, open but not too round, and bold without being black.

To those interested in printing types, as for the purpose of this discussion we must necessarily be, the type of the *De Aetna* (1495) offers a problem. Typefounding describes it as an "old face" or as a "venetian". It is, as a design, the direct progenitor of the letter-form we know by the nineteenth-century nickname of "old face" or "old style"; it is not a venetian, if Jenson's letter is typical of that school of type forms. The type of the *De Aetna* has little or nothing in common with the latter, and the point is worth stressing, because Venetian printing of the succeeding century gradually drew away from Jenson's model and, as we shall see, by 1560 was using almost exclusively a set of entirely different characters. The type of the *De Aetna* and of the beautiful *St. Katharine of Siena* gives a hint of this approaching change.

It may be noted that, from the time of his establishment as a printer until his death, Aldus never employed types which were immediately based on the Jenson model, nor did he employ them when, through marriage, much of Jenson's material came into his hands. Whether or not the Aldine letters are an improvement upon those of his illustrious predecessor is a matter of taste, but it will at least be agreed that they differ in many important respects. To our eyes they may claim to possess a much more "present day" feeling than is conveyed in the letters of the earlier master. The finest floriated initials give the *Poliphilus* a unique splendour; but it is unfortunate that Aldus, who published this work on commission and not as a venture of his own, should not have taken more pains with the production. The press-work is but average, and he made shift with at least two sets of initials, of which one series is demonstrably poor and inconsistent.

Though Aldus's merits as a fine printer have, like those of Jenson and Plantin, been exaggerated, his influence upon the printed book is certainly important. He began printing and publishing with great energy in 1495, and before the end of the century had printed some thirty-seven volumes, among them a five-volume Aristotle and other fine folios. His reputation, however, was made with books of smaller format. Aldus, indeed, wrought a remarkable change in publishing, and the *Poliphilus* is practically his last example of a large book. One of his literary friends, Urceus Codrus, wrote to Aldus in 1498, saying that he was pleased with the craftsmanship and accuracy of the Aristotle, but was indignant at the price. He added that with the money paid for Aldus's five volumes he could have purchased ten of the largest and best MSS. in Latin. Aldus's answer to this was the octavo series begun in 1501; and here we have at once the inception of the modern book and the modern publishing method.

The type of the *De Aetna* equally marks the new epoch in typography. The fame of the publisher added to the prestige of the new letter. It was copied in France (by Garamond, Colines and others), and later made its reappearance in Venice cast from French punches and with an added note of conscious elegance and technical perfection. The Jenson letter was no match for this newcomer, and we soon find that the taste of Venetian printers preferred these French copies and the French manner of display. Aldus's sons, for instance, are to be found using them in 1550. Thus Italian and French typography merged in the stream of that vigorous "old face" tradition which took its rise from the type of the Aldine *De Aetna*, and, as we shall see, suffered temporary eclipse during the eighteenth and nineteenth centuries, but which renewed its youth and strength under Pickering, until at the present day we find it dominating the finest typography of two continents. But this is to anticipate.

In spite of the illustrious and unique *Poliphilus*, Aldus was not greatly interested in typographical decoration. His work is, in the main, without ornament. As has been said, it is perhaps the case that Aldus has been over-praised. His reputation largely rests upon the cursive letter of Francesco Griffo, which he was the first to employ, and the octavo classics set in this letter, which are very workman-like volumes, thus gave the cursive a European advertisement. But there was another variety of cursive, based on the more formal chancery hand of the writing masters, which had its importance in the history of italic type. Lodovico degli Arrighi da Vicenza was employed at Rome as a "scrittore de' brevi apostolici" and as a writing master he was the first to print specimens of his hand. From 1524 to 1527 he was a printer at Rome, using two founts of italic of greater distinction and formality than the Aldine model. Their influence can be traced among other Italian printers and also at Paris. Arrighi's first fount was secured by Janiculo at Vicenza and the second fount passed to the Roman printer, Antonio Blado. Blado was a connection of Aldus and became papal printer in 1545, a position which he held until his death in 1567. Many of the productions of his press are notable and one or two are quite remarkable. His press early discerned the uses of the floret, and later of those units which combine to form arabesque ornaments (printers' flowers). Blado maintained his individual style throughout his career. His sons, however, were, like other Italian printers, obviously influenced by the charming title-pages to the productions of perhaps the most prolific of the sixteenth-century Venetian presses, that of the Gioliti. These volumes, in spite of their inferiority to the work, say, of Ratdolt, possess many points of interest. The Gioliti were, for instance, one of the earliest Italian houses to use printers' flowers. In the matter of decoration the craft is less indebted than might be imagined to Venetian inspiration. As I have previously remarked, the Ratdolt influence had borne no fruit and the appropriate typographical decoration of the printed page remained a problem—and, since it is human to decorate—an urgent problem.

The primitive impulse to decorate was followed by a satisfaction equally natural—the flowers and the leaves of the wayside became the simple ornament of the building, the table or the person. They found their inevitable echo in plastic art with its conventional garland and festoon, and the ornament won its way into every handicraft; the papyrus, the manuscript and finally the printed page is so adorned. The Venetian printers were rather slow in transferring decoration in the current taste to wood or metal blocks, and the first decorated title-page, that to Müller's *Kalender* published by Ratdolt in 1478, did not interest his fellow-craftsmen sufficiently to secure many imitators. In this matter Ratdolt, the son of a carpenter and woodcarver, was in advance of his time, and the rich borders of his Appian remain strangely isolated examples. His colleagues contented themselves with allowing the professional illuminators to decorate the printed sheets; and thus the principles of typographical decorations were somewhat tardily developed in spite of their considerable public interest.

The twofold inheritance of Venice as a leading renaissance city and the commercial gateway to the east brought with it a skill in two modes of floral decoration, the naturalistic form derived from classical art and the conventional form imported from the Mahommedan east. Ratdolt's decorative work affords examples of both these. His *Kalender* bears a particularly fine classical floral border, while the opening page of the Appian already referred to is framed in a border of conventional entre-lacs. In varying forms, but by no means at once, these two streams of ornament overflow the typography and book decoration of the fifteenth and sixteenth centuries.

Italy gave Europe the finest type forms, the finest decorations and the finest printing-papers of the fifteenth century, but its primacy in two most important points was destined to be lost in the early years of the sixteenth. It was from France that the printed book was next to receive its formative influences.

## IV

The printing of France, of course, owes its introduction to travelling German craftsmen. Strangely, they began with a type of the Roman kind, but the strength of public opinion in favour of the older style brought them back to the black letter. In one form or another the gothic type with appropriately heavy ornament ruled until the generation of Jodocus Badius and the first of the Estiennes. Henri of this dynasty, like his contemporaries, first used gothic derived types and ornaments, which he discarded when, like so many lesser men in Florence, Paris, Lyons and Basle, he yielded to the profitable temptation of copying Aldus. This was but a temporary phase, however. The first distinctly French contribution to the makings of the fine book was not delayed for long. The period during which the work of the best Parisian printers, Henri and Robert Estienne and Simon de Colines, exhibited obvious evidences of external influences, first of Venice and secondly of Basle, was succeeded by a time of great local enthusiasm for the renaissance which, rapidly assimilated by the French Church and the court, brought a new skill into the Arts and Crafts, and to printing a native style. By 1525 the French renaissance,

though originally Italian in almost every line, possessed a
soul of its own. The work of designers, craftsmen and decorators
imported from Italy by Francis I, penetrated architecture
and the handicrafts. In book production, however, it was a
native-born genius who effected in an incredibly short time
that change from the gothic type and decoration to the roman
type which it took almost two hundred years to do in England.
The work of Geofroy Tory marks a new epoch in printing. He
was a many-sided genius, a typical renaissance scholar. Originally lecturer in philosophy and sometime reader in the offices
of Gilles de Gourmont and Henri Estienne, his enthusiasm for
typography and the graphic arts led him to experiment with
printing and publishing. A prolonged sojourn in Italy greatly
affected him; after publishing with Simon de Colines, he established himself as bookseller, engraver and printer, and he became
the most powerful European influence in these crafts. Hence-
forth the work of the Parisian press is composed in lighter
faces of type and correspondingly lighter wood-engraved
illustrations. The heavy types, initials and borders derived
from Basle and used by Jodocus Badius were discarded by his
son-in-law successor, Michel Vascosan, in favour of Tory's
criblé initials and graceful entrelacs.

Many other fine printers followed the new taste, and Tory
gathered round him a number of craftsmen whom he trained
in the method of the finest Italian wood-engravers, achieving
nevertheless an individual note in his style. To pure typography
as to book-illustration his contributions were epoch marking,
if indirect. He was a great enthusiast for pure roman letter. He
made two or three sets of ornamental initial letters related in
design and colour to the type of the page and to the head-piece.
He was a most fertile creator of floral evolutions, of which he
made beautiful use in title-pages, borders and decorations. Thus
the Pot Cassé was the symbol of a new spirit in printing. Indebted as he was to Italy, Tory was not a slavish imitator, as is

proved by his *Heures* of 1525. It is not in the least surprising that the office of Imprimeur du roy in the French language was created for him in 1530. The leading Parisian printers of a later day strove to continue Tory's styles and the craft used his blocks for almost a generation after his death. The typefounder, Claude Garamond, became a figure of prime importance. The early cursives of Colines, which are derived partly from Aldus and partly from Arrighi, are probably his own work; and an enthusiasm for the type of the *Poliphilus* evidently prompted the cutting of the types used in the *Terentianus* of 1531. In the year 1530, a succession of strikes resulted in the separation of typefounding from printing, and Garamond established himself as a founder. After his death his types were sold to Plantin and others in the Low Countries, while Guillaume Le Bé was at Venice, and another pupil, Robert Granjon, carried the Garamond designs and his own italics to Florence and Rome. Types in these designs duly appeared in England and Spain, and in a few years French fashions dominated the whole of European typography, and initiated that powerful tradition which lives in William Caslon's so-called "old face", cut *circa* 1725. After Denys Janot, Parisian printing became obviously inferior to that of Lyons. The next creative impulse came from this city, which had early given a welcome to the craft but whose style, having fallen for a period under the influence of Basle, evolved a character of its own *circa* 1540.

In spite of the distinction given to the Basle press by the competence of Froben, the cuts of Holbein and a series of bold types, the city did not long retain any importance as a centre of printing style. Its affinities were German, and though a number of admirable books in the Basle style were put forth, its influence, though at first strongly exerted upon early Parisian and Lyonnese craftsmen, was temporary. Geofroy Tory's achievement rapidly overcame it. The latter's floriated headbands and initials were carried wherever the victorious Garamond letters were called for. Antwerp with Plantin, Frankfurt with the Egenolffs and the Wechels, and, of course, most of Switzerland and Italy came under the spell of the Parisian fashion. The national characteristics which had been so consistent a feature of the manuscripts gave way before the success of Tory's solution of the problem confronting every printer, that of uniting the type and the decoration in one colour, in one weight, and, if possible, in one convention. In many parts of the Continent and particularly Holland the imitations of Tory's style flourished for generations. We find them a consistent feature in that very overrated series, the 12mo Elzevirs, copied indeed, but without yielding the slightest pleasure.

In France, however, a fine solution of the same problem was worked out in another convention by the great Lyonnese printer Jean de Tournes, in association with the wood-engraver Bernard Salomon. Some of the printers of this city have earned a reputation for their unscrupulous imitation of Venetian models. The enterprise of Jean de Tournes, however, went far beyond this; and to him we owe a number of the very finest achievements of printing.

Jean de Tournes I was born in Lyons in 1504, and was apprenticed to the Trechsels. Afterwards he became foreman to Sebastian Gryphius, whose brother Francis had for some time worked in Paris. To what extent de Tournes was inspired by Tory's work it is not possible to say. It is, however, to the hand of Bernard Salomon that de Tournes was indebted for the marvellous arabesques which give his editions such notable distinction. Colines' 1543 *Book of Hours* includes a number of borders in precisely the same convention, but *le petit Bernard* (as he was known) carried it to an even finer conclusion. Thus, there appeared in French typography beautiful large floating fleurons such as those in the *Marguerites*. Though many of these afterwards appeared in Paris, their usage was invariably finer in Lyonnese work. They represent indeed a contribution to standard typographical decoration of the very first importance and that in a double degree. *Le petit Bernard's* preoccupation with the arabesque, his interest in engraving, and a family connection with one of the finest of all typefounders, Robert Granjon, perhaps assisted the latter to carry further the idea of placing decorative units upon type bodies which may be found in its simplest form in the title-pages of Antonio Blado of Rome from about 1530, and which there were copies of binders' tools. Granjon transformed the simple and complete *petit-fer* into a unit which would admit of the most marvellous combinations. This happy invention was, however, not too quickly received in France. Some varieties were used in Lyons and others in Paris, but it was in Venice, in Antwerp, in Frankfurt, in Nuremberg, in Rome, and in London, that they received the heartiest welcome. In the Netherlands, Granjon's dexterity was especially appreciated. The poet Van Vaernewyck of Gand, for instance, writes that Granjon "has as many ingenious ideas as hairs to his head", and he adds that he has seen a glorious arabesque as large as a man's hand made up from forty-eight pieces.

Examples of these interesting ornaments occur in work executed in Antwerp; rich and pleasant as these are, the eye is perhaps even better pleased by a series Granjon cut later and which are put to magnificent use by the brothers Le Preux, first at Paris, then at Lausanne and finally at Geneva.

Christopher Plantin holds a foremost position among the great printers of the past. It should be remarked at once, however, that his eminence is due more to his great activity as a publisher. At the same time it must be conceded that Plantin was not the man to rest content with accepted methods of book illustration, no matter how honoured by time and school. He was one of the first to extend the use of printers' flowers which had recently arrived in Antwerp. Plantin secured large supplies of fresh varieties, thus giving notable support to a fashion which

C

long endured in England. Plantin's later intimacy with the artists of the Low Countries led him first to commission wood-cut borders in the current and fast decaying renaissance style. Later he employed the engraved plate, to which he gave very extensive use. The engraved title-page quickly became a European vogue, spreading at once to France and even to England, at that time a backwater in printing. Plantin's affection for copper engravings did not stop at the title-page. He engaged the foremost artists and practitioners to design and execute the illustrations to the liturgical books, a patent for which he had secured in 1565. His books, unfortunately, exhibit a distinct tendency towards excessive decoration. Plantin was far from possessing that exact sense of values which characterises so many fine books issued in Paris and Lyons from 1520 to 1570. In fact, it would not be too much to say that as a printer Plantin has not merely been over-written but overrated. The truth is that Plantin editions are more distinguished by their number than by their typography. Before Plantin's arrival there were already in Antwerp several printers the excellence of whose work is certainly not surpassed by that of the newcomer. The fine madrigal books of Jean Bellère (with whose assistance Plantin was to issue his first book) come readily to the memory. There were also smaller printing shops where fine work was done. Such was the office of Jean Loe, who printed many of the theological and philosophical disputations for the University of Louvain, then, as now, the headquarters of scholasticism. Still another worthy Antwerp printer was Stelsius, who, in spite of his rather mean Bible, wrought well and consistently in a number of pretty little volumes. When Plantin arrived in 1554 he found Antwerp printing already prosperous and distinguished, and it cannot justly be said that he raised its aesthetic standards.

## V

That sixteenth-century printing is indebted to France for several most important developments is clear. In the meanwhile Italian typography had sunk to a low level, and it must be confessed that by the end of the same century, though the best printing in Europe was still French, it marked a great declension from the golden age of Tory and the Estiennes. In the seventeenth century, France, after almost two generations of uninteresting and careless work, was to renew its enthusiasm and endeavour. There are signs of this by the year 1640, when Richelieu was able to persuade Louis XIII to establish a royal printing-house, from which the State documents and certain other works could be published.

Richelieu's interest in typography dated probably from his appointment to the direction of a privileged group who printed missals, breviaries and other liturgical works. The Cardinal later extended the work of the group to cover the printing of the New Testament, catechisms, and grammars of oriental languages for the use of missionaries in the Levant. It would appear that the concerted action of this society of some eighteen printers failed to realise the hopes which Richelieu had conceived. However it may have been, in 1639 the Cardinal persuaded Louis XIII to establish a press in the Louvre. On November 17th, 1640, the Imprimerie Royale, or Typographia Regia, commenced work under the direction of Sébastien Cramoisy. Its first publication was a handsome folio text of the *De Imitatione Christi*. It is printed in types after the Garamond design, but its merits are somewhat compromised by the insipid copper-plate vignettes of Nicolas Poussin, whom Richelieu induced to leave Italy and to reside in the precincts of the Louvre. In 1642 Richelieu's own book *Principaux points de la foi* was set in new types acquired from Jean Jannon of Sedan.

These romans and italics were named "caractères de l'Université" and were, in the nineteenth century, wrongly assigned to Garamond, to the confusion of typographic historians. In rather royal and leisurely fashion the press proceeded to bring out a number of imposing folios. At this period its work was sufficiently well handled to arouse the envious interest of printers abroad. An interesting evidence of foreign endeavour to secure supplies of French types is afforded by a Royal Decree of March 25th, 1642. This enactment forbids booksellers, printers, typefounders and all other persons of whatsoever quality to vend or convey to foreigners matrices or founts of any kind, under a penalty of 1000 livres. This order seems to have secured obedience. In 1663, however, Ant. Estienne was found to have sold a fount of the Royal Greek to one Lucas, who purveyed them to Jean Berthelin, a Rouen merchant in touch with foreign booksellers. The types were at once seized and Estienne mulcted in a fine.

This incident indicates the growing jealousy with which the King and his Ministers watched over the Crown types. It is therefore not surprising that with the death of Sébastian Mabre-Cramoisy (grandson and successor of the first director) and the accession of Jean Anisson to the directorate of the royal press in 1691, there should have been suggested the creation of an entirely new set of roman types. It was proposed that the use of this letter be absolutely reserved to the Louvre. Monsieur de Pontchartrain, Court Chancellor, favoured the project, and in 1692 Louis XIV sanctioned it.

The enterprise was undertaken with remarkable deliberation. A commission of experts appointed by the Académie Royale des Sciences set to work excogitating and codifying rules for the formation of perfect roman letter. The chairman of the commission, one Jaugeon, embodied its findings in a bulky report which even now lies unprinted. Attached to the report are a number of elaborate geometric designs in which the traditional roman form was submitted to the discipline of the rule and compasses. The letters were drawn upon a square which subdivided into no fewer than 2304 small squares. The royal road to a perfect roman letter was, therefore, a mathematical one. This was well enough for the patterns which were ordered to be transferred to copper by the elder Simonneau, one of the finest engravers of the day. Philippe Grandjean, however, to whom had been committed the task of punch-cutting, elected to work with a considerable degree of independence.

Treating Simonneau's plates merely as valuable suggestions, Grandjean preferred the guidance of his own trained eye. His variations from Jaugeon's standard are consequently not unimportant. The *romain du roi Louis XIV*, as the new letter was called, remained a distinct novelty. In comparison with Garamond's roman it displays a sharper contrast between its thick and thin strokes, and is also more regular and more mechanically perfect, *i.e.* better in its justification. The most important general difference, however, is in respect to serif. For the first time the thin, flat unbracketed variety was employed and on the top of the roman lower-case ascenders the new feature extended both sides.

The royal monopoly of the *romain du roi* was safeguarded by the enactment of penalties against its reproduction by trade typefounders. In the meantime Grandjean and his assistants, Jean Alexandre and Louis Luce, were cutting it in many sizes. In 1702 the Imprimerie Royale issued its first specimen, displaying the *romain du roi* in a large variety of bodies. As the stocks of the new letter increased, the "old face" of Garamond was superseded. The first publication (*i.e.* apart from the specimen just mentioned) to employ the *romain du roi* was a volume issued in 1702: *Médailles sur les évènements du règne de Louis-le-Grand*. This work is a magnificent folio and reaches the very highest pitch of craftsmanship. The book, as we learn from the preface, was begun in 1694. It has an engraved frontispiece by the elder Simonneau after Coypel *fils*; its borders and fleurons are by that prince of decorators, Berain; the head of the king on the medals is from the burin of Gerard. As for the types, they were "nouveaux, dessinez, gravez et fondus par le sieur Grandjean".

The *Médailles* is undoubtedly the most splendid example of the ornate and sophisticated book. It provides a most distinguished first setting forth of the *romain du roi*. Grandjean's improved justification and the novel cut of his type sorted most consistently with the Berain borders, the silky hand-made paper and the cut of the medals; the volume was a popular no less than an artistic success. The quarto edition was issued in the same year to content the interest of the public; Coypel's frontispiece and the medals were retained, and a smaller face of Grandjean was employed for the body of the work. In spite of its comparative plainness this edition also found a ready sale and a third was needed. The *romain du roi* instantly captivated the taste of the book-buyer; by 1714, when Grandjean died, there had been cut some twenty-one sizes, of which the chief punch-cutter had himself accounted for fifteen. The booksellers, printers and typefounders of Paris were now face to face on the one hand with a change in the public taste and on the other a royal decree forbidding any counterfeiting of the new face. The *goût nouveau* had to be satisfied with as great an approximation to Louis XIV's types as would escape the vindication of the law. Thus was the way paved for compromise. The leading Parisian typefounders slowly recut their capitals in the new mode and refined somewhat their lower-case roman. As to the cursive, the founders (and notably Fournier in 1737) were more bold, producing a letter almost identical with that of Grandjean. Concurrently with the change of type fashion initiated by the letters of Louis XIV the public taste, stimulated by the luxury of the baroque and rococo styles, grew to demand abundance and variety of adornment in its books. The luxurious appetite of the Court established the *livre de luxe* as one of the essential extravagances. The letter-press of the printer, therefore, joined with the rolling-press of the engraver, to produce the sumptuous and fascinating works illustrated by such masters as Nicolas Cochin and J. M. Moreau-le-jeune.

Though the Elzevirs since 1630 had produced their dull duodecimos, there had been issued in Paris few books to relieve the everlasting folio and quarto. The very dexterity of the illustrators in *taille-douce* tended to keep the French book in a size no smaller at least than octavo. Smaller books, however, were not now long in coming from the French presses. The most prominent of the Parisian typefounders, Pierre Simon Fournier, brought out *Modèles des caractères de l'imprimerie nouvellement gravés par P. S. Fournier*, in oblong folio, 1742: this contains a number of faces in the new taste, and a vast number of fleurons and vignettes-de-fonte which, as Luce had shown, could be built up into the festoons and borders, head- and tail-pieces, beloved of the period. With Fournier's devices it became possible for printers to produce a charming book with less recourse to the copper-plate. Head-pieces formerly commissioned from the engraver gave place to bouquets of Fournier's flowers, or to the convenient woodcuts of Papillon and his pupils. Slowly the eighteenth-century book underwent a change. The typefounders marketed their plain and decorated initials and a variety of *caractères de fantaisie*, imitated from the hands affected by the engravers. The dainty 12mo series of classical authors begun by Francis de la Tour in 1743, later bought up by Barbou, the handy volumes issued by Prault, uncle of Moreau-le-jeune, assisted public appreciation of the small volume. In time spared from his work at the Louvre, Luce cut some fifteen sizes during the years 1740 to 1770. These types, entitled the *Poétiques*, with a large number of new ornaments and borders, were purchased for the considerable sum of 100,000 livres by Louis XV in 1774. The *Poétiques* represent the first attempt in France to found a condensed letter. They of course owe little to Garamond, and are indeed too ugly to be shown in these pages. It should be added that Dutch and German founders had for some years been experimenting with space-saving types, types of a large x height; witness the work of Anton Janson, a Dutchman who founded at Leipzig, and the series of surviving types which have been given the name of "Janson".

Luce's types linked with the future Didot and Bodoni types, of which European printing was far too long patient. About 1780, François Ambroise Didot, first of a great dynasty of printers, caused to be cut a roman and cursive which show an increased contrast between the thicks and thins, a hair-line serif and condensed capitals; and at least two generations of readers came to accept this as the typical French face. The French Revolution naturally assisted a break, even with the typographical past. Ornaments and decoration were dropped as propaganda of the *ancien régime*. The cold, widely spaced and leaded pages of Baskerville, which had been copied by G. B. Bodoni, the renowned printer of Parma, were popularised in France by the Didots and a complete abandonment of the old faces resulted. In 1790, Bodoni himself cut a type heavier in weight, but whose contour was in the main identical with that of the Firmin Didot 1775.

Meanwhile printing abroad was corruptly following French fashions; Dutch printers reproduced more or less exactly the characteristics of French typography. English printers, even of the sixteenth century with superb achievements of French colleagues before their eyes, seldom rose above the commonplace, and the promise of the pretty title-pages of Denham and Bynneman is not fulfilled in the body of their books. The fair pitch of craftsmanship reached in the early part of the seventeenth century was ruined by the civil war. "Fine" printing therefore began late in England. The beginning of a style at once national and fine can be discerned in the work of the University presses of Oxford and Cambridge and, in London, in the enterprise of the elder Bowyer, and the development of sound English type-faces brought to our craftsmen the raw material of fine printing. It was the letter and, above all, the style of John Baskerville's books which emancipated our printers from the habit of imitating, albeit corruptly, the current heavy Dutch fashions in typography. Now, for the first time, English printing became an influence in Europe. Baskerville was the first who not merely freed himself from that tutelage to Continental printing which had been our characteristic since the time of Caxton, but was himself to influence profoundly the whole course of subsequent typography, both English and Continental. With his open round letters, widely spaced upon luxurious paper of his own invention, and exaggerated margins, his work astonished his English contemporaries and immensely interested his foreign colleagues.

Foremost among the latter was Bodoni, who had been appointed printer to the Court of Parma in the year 1768. When he first began to print, Bodoni employed the characters and ornaments of Fournier and produced several delightful specimens with this material. Likely enough it was Baskerville's 1773 edition of Ariosto's *Orlando Furioso*, handsomely printed in Italian, which excited the admiration of Bodoni. Accordingly, within the next few years Bodoni is to be found widely leading his pages and in other directions following the Baskerville model. In his type form, however, Bodoni remained faithful to the narrower-bodied letters of Grandjean and Fournier. Bodoni, however, cut several series of his own design; he strengthened the thick lines and refined the thins, thus producing that sharpness of contrast which, exaggerated by the brilliance of his impression and the luxury of his paper, seduced every European typographer from allegiance to the more soundly built letters of obviously finer design known to printers as the "old faces".

Thus Paris was at last surpassed in typographical prestige by
Bodoni if not by Baskerville. The typography of the French
Revolution is often handsome and striking, but its inspiration
is to be traced in the work done in Birmingham twenty years
before. In the nineteenth century the Didots carried on the
Bodoni tradition and certainly made a much finer use of it
than Bodoni's Italian successors. A really fine period in English
work opened with the closing decades of the eighteenth century.
The interest created by Baskerville had been further excited
when Bodoni printed books for Horace Walpole, whose Strawberry Hill Press itself encouraged interest in typography. Much
finer work, however, was produced by John Bell, Bensley,
Bulmer, Johnson (of the *Typographia*) and others. It is in fact
no exaggeration to say that the years 1770 to 1820 represent
the finest period of English typography. It was characterised
by extremely simple use of standard material, and high technical craftsmanship. The style, though it reminds us from time
to time of Baskerville and Bodoni, is undeniably native in
character and it represents the end of an epoch. The work of
John Bell, however, should be excepted, in that he was a
pioneer in typographic history. When he established his
British Letter Foundry with Richard Austin as punch-cutter he
began a new tradition in English type design. Bell and Austin's
types were clearly derived from the new Didot types of 1783-
1784, and proved to be the beginning of the type-founding
style known as "modern" face, the predominant style of the
nineteenth century and well into the twentieth.


VI


Here it becomes important to emphasise that the changes in
printing style which had passed over the craft since the days of

Jenson had been slow and gradual in their development. It may be well, too, to remark that there have been few entirely bad periods during the centuries, but long periods of good typography and bad machining, and of fair decoration and bad types, and so on. At last some conscientious and instructed craftsman impels his fellows by his own example to higher efforts. Thus a better period opens and printing gradually improves. It has been observed that the principal changes in book production are associated with the names of Jenson, Aldus, Tory, Grandjean, Fournier, Baskerville, Bodoni. Now must be added the name of Pickering, a publisher who designed his books; and here a change of high significance is to be noted.

An entirely new attitude now shows itself, an attitude which is at the present day fast becoming distinctive of American and English fine book work. Pickering's experiments were made outside the bounds of the convention of his day; so far this is not very remarkable. Grandjean, who in 1702 equipped the Imprimerie Royale with a set of newly designed types, broke fresh ground. Baskerville, the Didots, Bodoni and Bell carried further his ideas. But, it is essential to remember, none dreamt of returning to the typography of a past age. It was reserved for Pickering to make a series of experiments which were inspired by the models of sixteenth-century Paris, Lyons and Basle. In the case of Pickering, however much we may admire the revived renaissance borders which gave distinction to his reprints of sixteenth-century divines like Jeremy Taylor and Joseph Hammond, it may be doubted whether their use is very appropriate. He is happier, one may think, in his undecorated volumes or in such experiments as Fuller's *Good Thoughts*, where he is influenced by the propaganda of Pugin. The gothic revival indeed has a number of interesting books to its credit. John Philip, for instance, produced more than one fine liturgical book, appropriately enough decorated in this fashion; and William Morris's own romanticism was no doubt but an extension of the interest in mediaevalism inevitably created by the Oxford Movement. Morris's preoccupation in this regard led him to see the printing of preceding generations from the standpoint of a somewhat impatient censor. The Kelmscott Chaucer is splendid in its conception, its ornament and its archaism.

The influence of Morris's work was enormous, but it is infinitely to be regretted that his enthusiasm for the Middle Ages led him to go behind the roman letter. The Golden type is his single contribution to its development, for which he might have done so much had he not been under the spell of the incunable. The Golden type is a barren achievement because the Kelmscott master had not realised that, though black is the ideal colour for a gothic age, the roman letter with its finer contour demands a different colour, and can be brought into conformity with gothic standards only by compromising its essential grace and form. So the Golden type is coarse and heavy in comparison with that of, say, Tory. William Morris's merits as a book decorator in the mediaeval manner, however, are unapproachable; but the present generation of amateurs and practitioners of typography owes him a greater debt than is represented by the great Kelmscott Chaucer and his other books. His passion for perfect craftsmanship and his whole-hearted application to detail are an enduring inspiration, and his energy, by focusing interest in the craft, has made possible much of the variety and excellence which characterise present-day typography. Progress has been slow, nevertheless, and greatly as Morris helped us, he might have done more had he been less blind to the merits of great printers of the previous generation, Martin, Bulmer and Bensley. Though he came immediately after Pickering his example distracted attention from the most permanent of the early Victorian's endeavours towards fine printing—his reversion to Caslon's so-called "old face" for title-pages, and later for text use. Morris's work, however, powerfully recommended printing to the interest of the public, and thus the trade was stimulated almost indeed against its will; and one or two establishments were soon to put forth efforts in the direction of improvement. The press of the University of Oxford, long content with the commonplace, produced under Horace Hart a number of careful productions, advancing later to several fine books in the Fell types, which Daniel had been for some years using in his individual and carefree way for the composition of small editions of poems by his friends. These last count rather as interesting than as fine printing, and it still remained for the University Press to make handsome use of this seventeenth-century material. In 1899 the *Yattendon Hymnal* appeared, printed by the interest of its editor in the Fell types and employing for the music the characters cast from the punches of Peter Walpergen, cut *circa* 1660. The title-page of the volume is decorated with arabesque flowers, of which Robert Bridges had made similar use for the first edition of his *New Poems*, published in 1874 by Basil Montagu Pickering. Other works by Bridges are decorated by happy combinations of the Fell flowers, but the most magnificent usage of this material is to be found in the two large quarto editions of the *Book of Common Prayer*, the fruit of the joint labours of Charles Cannan and Horace Hart. The competence of the press is, however, not limited to the expert handling of its unique seventeenth-century types, as is proved by a number of recent title-pages, some in Caslon "old face" and others in "modern".

Prominent among the public presses that drew inspiration from the Arts and Crafts movement is the Arden Press of Letchworth, and later, London, which, during the years 1904 to 1914, was distinguished by its fine use of Caslon types. The school of calligraphy founded by Edward Johnston may be counted among the influences upon the typography of the

Arden Press. The finest contribution from this school is, however, to be found in the productions of the Doves Press established in 1902, which employ a number of Johnston's initials of
splendid form and colour. These appear at their best in that
superb effort, the Doves Bible, produced by Emery Walker and
Cobden-Sanderson in 1903–5. In spite of the fact that the Doves
type suffers, as must all types directly based upon Jenson's, from
over-large capitals, the Bible represents the finest achievement
of modern English printing, and a standard to which subsequent
Doves books never attained. It may be admitted that others,
*e.g.* the *Sartor Resartus*, are simply bad books.

St. John Hornby's Ashendene Press is another private press
owing much to the calligraphic movement. His Dante is a
magnificent book, second in merit only to the Doves Bible.
The type used is a recutting of the first roman type that was
employed at Subiaco by Schweynheym and Pannartz.

Fine printing in America is a post-Morris development.
The Kelmscott Press began work in 1891, and it was in 1893
that Daniel Berkeley Updike established the Merrymount Press.
In addition to a large output of workaday volumes the press
has printed a number of special books of more immediate
interest to the collector of fine printing. Its early productions
in this field were conceived in the heavy style which Morris
had striven for even with his Golden types; but these were
followed by a series of reprints of humanistic writers, printed
with complete appropriateness in the style of the Italian renaissance, but in a rather inferior letter. Updike was fortunate, however, in having secured much the best of the Horne types. More
recently, Updike developed an enthusiasm for the period which
I have ventured to call the golden age of English printing:
the sub-Baskerville age or the period of Bulmer and Bensley.
He has contributed in a unique degree to the solution of the
problems that beset the modern typographer. Merrymount is
a press established not as a personal hobby subject to private

subsidy, but as a commercial undertaking uniquely directed—
by a printer singularly endowed with a ripe typographical
scholarship and those rare complements, practical capacity and
a discriminating susceptibility to the beautiful in all its forms.

Updike's equal, as scholar and designer, Bruce Rogers, has
worked in Europe as well as in America. His is a lively spirit
and his work exhibits the most remarkable versatility. Happily
uninfluenced by Morris's spirit, his books include a number of
fine inventions in every style from the Italian renaissance to
the French Directory. They are perfect examples of their kind,
and though, in a sense, the style of many of them is derivative,
they are all marked with the impress of his own personality.
Mr. Rogers knows better than anybody else how to make typographical form illustrate the literary content. He is, in fact, the
first of typographers, and not a printer at all. Hence he will only
design a book because he chooses to, whereas Updike would
design a book because it was brought to him. Perhaps the most
delightful of all the volumes in Mr. Rogers's diverse list is
the *Compleat Angler*. The typography, while "period", is supported by original decorations of the happiest kind, and the
title-page with its charming vignette, also by Mr. Rogers, is a
masterpiece.

The typographical history of the last two generations is a
study in revivals, notably in England and America; and abroad
also. The revival of "old face" type under Pickering and the
Whittinghams, for instance, has a parallel in France. A similar
movement was initiated by the publisher Louis Perrin, who in
1846 cut a series of letters with capitals directly based upon
the classical roman forms, and whose lower-case followed
somewhat the types of Garamond. This revival occasioned an
interest in old style printing and led a reaction against the
Didot manner. It had, nevertheless, a purely literary success, and
that a restricted one. The revived Lyons types were accom-
panied by a selection of decorations composed of conventional

renaissance flowers and grotesques, such as the Elzevirs had used
two centuries earlier, and the style became known as neo-
Elzevir. A number of pretty volumes was issued in this style—
the Jouaust and Lemerre series are known to all. The finest
work in Perrin's types is, however, to be found in that town
with which Lyons had always been closely connected, Geneva.
Here the press, directed first by Jules and later by Édouard Fick,
produced a large number of elegant reprints in the style of the
sixteenth century. The Fick press was the fortunate possessor
of a large number of the original wood-blocks cut for Jean de
Tournes by Bernard Salomon, and which the son conveyed with
him when he fled from Lyons. The blocks, it may be interesting
to record, remain in Geneva to this day.

In 1870 the printer, Jules Claye of Paris, recut a large number
of decorated initials, vignettes and fleurons in the arabesque
manner originally created by Peter Flötner of Nuremberg,
1546, and which were much used by Rouillé and Jean de
Tournes II. Collectors, however, of fine French printing dis-
cover little of interest in even the best years of the nineteenth
century. Volumes in which typographical ambition played any
part were dressed in either the neo-Elzevir or the neo-Lyons
style. These were hardly varied until the advent in 1896 of
Édouard Pelletan, who, that year, established the first publishing house in modern days to employ for secular purposes the
types of Jannon, Grandjean and Luce. Pelletan strove to con-
serve a very high standard, and in his several illustrated series
achieved many successes.

The twentieth century witnessed an awakening among
French bibliophiles. Pelletan's example was not without its
effect, and at the same time there succeeded to the direction of
the Imprimerie Nationale an erudite and practical enthusiast in
Arthur Christian. During his period of office (cut short by his
death in 1906), there was printed the immense work of Claudin,
*Histoire de l'imprimerie en France* (1900), composed in large sizes

of Jannon and Grandjean types. This monumental work was followed by several admirably printed monographs by Christian. Though private clubs, supported by powerful personages in society and politics, were devoting themselves to the printed book, the private press as known to English and German amateurs secured no lodgement in the ambitions of French enthusiasts, but the close understanding on the part of publishers with contemporary artists resulted in the execution of many interesting books illustrated with wood-engravings, *eaux fortes*, etc. But consideration of these obviously belongs rather to the amateur of illustration than typography.

The most satisfying examples of German typography will be found, I think, not among the productions of the numerous private presses established by enthusiastic admirers of the Doves Press, but among the more normal productions of public presses. In this connection the Insel-Verlag takes a prominent position, if only for its series of German classics entitled the Grossherzog Wilhelm Ernst Ausgabe, printed by Germany's finest typographer, Herr Carl Ernst Poeschel, and which began to appear in 1905. The format of the series was designed by Sir Emery Walker, and the volumes possess calligraphic title-pages designed by Johnston and by Eric Gill. The most successful German efforts are of recent completion and are unfortunately outside the scope of this volume; yet notice must be given to the admirable work of the Bremer Presse, a Munich establishment formed in 1914 by Dr. Wilhelm Wiegand. The original type designed by Dr. Wiegand is perhaps too large for the page, but the smaller size cut for a text of the *De Civitate Dei* is undoubtedly a successful type, in spite of one or two questionable characters. The Bremer books are invariably undecorated save for the handsome initials designed by Anna Simons. In no country is printing more seriously studied than in Germany, and if their typographers can cultivate freedom without compromising the essentially traditional

D

character of the craft, they will achieve perhaps our greatest desideratum: the reconciliation of the old craft with the spirit of modernism.

Much of the so-called "fine printing" from William Morris to Bruce Rogers (though the latter's most recent works are delightfully "modern") is an anachronism, and will never be singled out by the historian of the future as the representative printing of our period. Nevertheless it must be admitted that so much does almost every individual among us assist in the cult of the past, that to provide the mock antique is one of the surest ways to a reputation for fine printing. Yet this seems fundamentally wrong. To some of us it may be more exciting to play with sixteenth-century flowers, and to all of us it is easier to copy old styles than to make a good one of our own. It may even be urged that in printing, as perhaps in most things, all possible combinations have been exhausted; but French and German typographers do not think so. The French are never afraid to shock us by some new trick of display, nor the Germans to do so with a new type face. But these attempts are to the average English and American taste not derivative enough. They fail to respect many traditions and conventions which are so strong with us, and very extraordinary things have been achieved by some of the Teutonic private presses ignoring them. Gradually, however, they are learning moderation. One of the extremest men of a few years ago, Professor F. H. Ehmcke, though he never rivalled Monsieur Georges Auriol, has produced a series of books in a newly designed cursive which really does resemble a printing type; and today type must look like type.

We come back to the question of basic principles. If we are acting against the highest interests of typography by remaining content with resurrected Garamond, Aldus, Jenson, and period usages thereof, what is the next step? We must have new types, new ornaments (perhaps even new conventions of display can

be worked out) by the living rather than copies from the illustrious dead; therefore it is proper, indeed necessary, to study the
history of printing not as an end in itself, but as a means, an
inspiration towards the typographical task before us. We may
not obscure the old truths: we must not despise the new.

# CHRONOLOGICAL LIST OF PLATES

## XVI CENTURY SWITZERLAND, GERMANY AND THE LOW COUNTRIES

### *BASLE, ETC.*

# THE PLATES

*The size of the type area of the*
*original page is shown in*
*inches under each plate*

NSTITVENTI michi . Q . frater eū sermonē
referre & mandare huic tertio libro quē post an-
thonii disputationē crassus habuisset : acerba sane
'recordatio : ueterē animi curā molestiamq; reno-
uauit. Nam illud imortalitate dignū ingemū : illa
humanitas : illa uirtus. L. crassi morte exticta subito est : uixit diebus decem post eū diem q̄ hoc et superiore
libro cōtinet. Vt eni romam rediit extremo scenicox ludox
die uehementer cōmotus : ea oratione que ferebat habita esse
i cōcione a philippo quē dixisse constabat uidendū sibi esse
aliud cōsiliū : illo senatu se rē. p. regere nō posse : mane idibq
septembris. et ille et senatus frequēs uocatu drusi in curiam
uenit . Ibi cū drusi multa de philippo questus esset : retulit
ad senatū de illo ipo quod in eū ordinē consul tam grauiter
in cōcione esset iniectus. Hic ut sepe inter hoies sapiēnssimos
constare uidi quāq̄ hoc crasso : cū aliquid accuratius dixis-
set semp fere cōtigisset : ut nūq̄ dixisse melius putaret : tamē
omniū consensu sic esse tum iudicatū audiui ceteros a crasso
semp omnes illo autē die enā ipm a sese supatū. Deplorauit
eni casum atq; orbitatē senatus cuius ordinis a consule qui
quasi parēs bonus aut tutor fidelis esse deberet : tanq̄ ab ali-
quo nefario predone diriperet patrimoniū dignitatis. Neq;
q; uero inq̄t esse mirādum si tum suis cōsiliis rem. p. p̄fli-
gasset. cōsiliū senatus rei. p. repudiaret. Hic cum homini et
uehemēti et diserto et in p̄mis forti ad resistendum philippo
quasi quasdā uerbox faces admouisset : nō tulit ille : et grauiter exarsit pignoribusq; ablatis crassū istituit cohercere.

Cicero: *De Oratore*

Subiaco: Schweynheym and Pannartz, 1465

$7'' \times 4\frac{1}{8}''$

E

corporibus induunt:numina uocant:quae in spiritu accepto subito occurrerēt
monstra haberentur.Deinde aliquāto post cum theologiā naturalē predicans
quorundam philosophorum sentētias digessisset:opposuit sibi questionē &
ait.Hoc loco dicit aliquis.Credat ergo cęlum & terram deos esse:& supra lunā
alios:infra alios.Ego feram aut Platonem aut peripateticum Stratonē:quoꝗ
alter deum fecit sine corpore:alter sine animo.Et ad hoc respondens qd ergo
tandem inquit?Veriora uidentur Titi Titii aut Romuli:aut Tulli Hostilii
summa:Cloatinam Titus Tatius dedicauit:deam Picum Tiberinūꝗ Rōulus
Hostilius Pauorem atꝗ Pallorem:teterrimos hominum affectus:quoꝗ alter
mentis territę motus ē alter corp oris:ne morbus quidē sed color. Hęc numia
potius credes & cęlo recipies:De ipsi uero ritibus crudeliter turpibus ꝗ libere
scripsit.Ille inquit utriles sibi partes amputat: ille lacertos secat. Vbi iratos
deos timent qui sic propicios mirentur:Di autem nullo debent coli genere:
si & hęc uolunt.Tantus est perturbatę metis & sedibus suis pulsę furor:ut sic
dii placentur quemadmodum ne quidem homines sęuiunt teterrimi: & in
fabulas traditi crudelitatis . Tiranni lacerauerunt aliquorum membra ne
minem sua lacerare iusserunt . Regię libidinis uoluptati castrati sunt quidā
sed nemo sibi ne uir est& iubente domino manus intulit . Se ipsi in templis
contrucidant:uulneribus suis ac sanguine supplicant.Si cui iubeti uacet quę
faciunt quęꝗ patiuntur:inueniet tam indecora honestis:tam indigna liberis
tam dissimilia sanis:ut nemo fuerit dubitaturus furere eos.Si cū paucioribus
furerent utcunꝗ ferendi essent:nunc sanitatis patrocinium est isaniēū turca
Iam illa quę ipso capitolio fieri solere commemorat:& intrepide omnino co
arguit:quis credat nisi ab irridētibus aut furentibus fieri? Nam cum in sacris
ęgyptiis Osyri lugeri perditū:mox autem de inuento magnum tuisse gaudiū
derisus& cum perditio eius inuentioꝗ fingatur:dolor tamen ille atꝗ laeticia
ab eis qui nihil perdiderūt nihilꝗ inuenerunt ueraciter exprimat: huic tamē
inquit furori certum tempus est. Tolerabile est semel in anno insanire i capi
tolū peruenire.Pudebit publicatę demetię:ꝗa quod sibi uinai furor attribuit
officii:alius nomina deo subicit:alius horas Ioui nūtiat:alius lictor est : alius
uctor qui uano motu brachiorum imitatur ungentem.Sunt quę Iunoni ac
Mineruae capillos disponant:longe a tēplo non tantum a simulachro stātes
digitos mouent ornātium modo:sunt quae speculum teneant:sunt quae ad
uadimonia sua deos aduocent:sunt qui libellos offerant & illos cautam suam
doceant. Doctus Archiminus senex uam decrepitus : quottidie in capitolio
mimum agebat:quasi dii libenter expectarent:quem illi homines deserrant.
Omne illic artificum genus operantium dns immortalibus desid&.Et paulo
post.Hi tamen inquit etiam si superuacuum usum:non turpem nec infamē
deo promittunt.Sedent quędam in capitolio quę se a Ioue amari putant : nec
Iunonis quidem si credere poetis uelis iracudissime respectu terentur.Hāc
libertatem Varro non habuit tantummodo poeticam theologiā repręhēdere
ausus e:ciuilē nō ausus ë:quā iste cōcidit:Sed si uerę attēdius deteriora sūt tēpla
ubi hęc aguntur:ꝗ theatra ubi finguntur. Vnde ī his sacris ciuilis theologiae
has partes potius elegit Seneca sapiens:ut eas in animi religione non habeat
sed in actibus fingat.Ait enim quę omnia sapiens seruabat tāꝗ legibus iussa
nō tāꝗ diis grata.Et paulopost.Quid ꝗ & matrimonia inquit deoꝗ stūgus
& ne pie quidem fratrum scilicet & sororum? Bellonam Marti collocamus
Vulcano Venerem.Neptuno Salaciam.Quosdam tamen celibes relinꝗmus
quasi condicio defecerit prefertim cum quę tam uiduę sint:ut Populonia uel
Fulgora:et diua Rumina quibus non miror petitorem defuisse.Omnem istā

Augustinus: *De Civitate Dei*

Subiaco: Da Spira, 1470

$10\frac{5}{8}'' \times 5\frac{3}{4}''$

cætera. Hio hias ex quo iteratiuum figuratur hiato: hiatas.
Inchoatiuum uero figuratur hifco hifcis cum dicimus.
Sed quanq̃ ita fe habeant tamen plus effe uidetur i eoquod
é hifcei q̃ hiare. Hiat eim qui ore patet uel tacitus tm̄ quod
in rebus fictis animaduerti pot. hifcere uero incipere loqui.
Illud præterea nōnullis libuit animaduertere q̃ actiuis acti
ua nōnulla figurata ichoatiua ſperiūtur etiā paſſiua: quale
é gelo gelas: cuius inchoatiuum facit gelafco quod é ſcipio
gelare.
Item cum é lento lentas: Vnde Virgilius: Lentandus remus i
unda. Ex hoc inchoatiuum lentefco facit ut idem Virgilius
Et picis in morem ad digitos lentefcit habendo. Eiufmodi
figuratio parum admiſit ex fe perfectum: nec conuenit ad
mittere ut aut poſſit: aut debeat cum cæteris temporibus p
totam declinationem uim incipiendi fignificare. Abſurdū
é ergo ea quæ funt inchoatiua perfecto tempore definire: &
mox futurum declinando inchoatiua effe demōftrare· Nec
enim pote.̃t cum tota uerbi fpecies inchoatiua dicatur alia
parte finitiua uiden ut perfectum admittat. Nec enim pale
fciui: horrefciui dicimus. per aliam tamen tranſfigurationē
hæc uerba quidam declinare confueuerunt. ut palefco: pale
factus fum: liquefco liquefactus fum. quāuis quidam ad p
fectum inchoatiuum uenerint modo primitiui ut horrefco
horrui ex eo quod é horreo. Nec tamen omnia inchoatiua
habent primam pofitionem. Albefco enim nō habet albeo
licet figuranter Virgilius: Campiq; ſgentes offibus albent.
Item putrefco: grādefco: ſiluefco: uilefco: brutefco: iuuene
fco nō habet iuueneo. Nam fenefco & feneo apud ātiquos
dicebarur. Vnde & Catullus nunc recondita fenet.
Deducuntur item inchoatiua a neutris uerbis & appellationi
bus. ex uerbis: ut caleo calefco: deliteo delitefco: fródeo fró
defco: floreo florefco. Et funt hæc quæ a perfecta forma ue
niūt. Sūt ité quæ origiñe fui nō habet: ut cōfuefco: cōquie
fco. Sunt quoq; alia inchoatiuis fimilia quæ inchoatiua nō
effe temporum confideratione pernofcimus. ut compefco

Diomedes: *De Arte Grammatica*

Subiaco: Jenson, 1480

$7\frac{1}{2}'' \times 4\frac{3}{8}''$

Herodotus

Subiaco: Ioannes & Gregorius de Gregoriis, 1494

$11\tfrac{3}{4}'' \times 7\tfrac{3}{4}''$

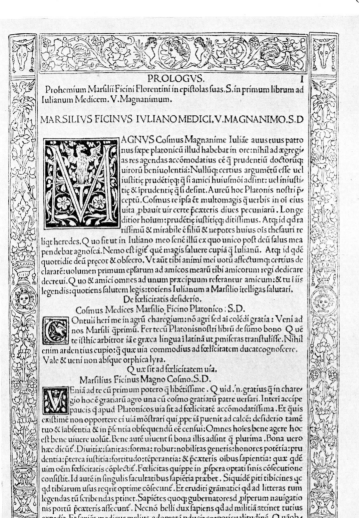

### PROLOGVS.                                                          I

Prohemium Marsilii Ficini Florentini in epistolas suas. S. in primum librum ad
Iulianum Medicem. V. Magnanimum.

MARSILIVS FICINVS IVLIANO MEDICI, V. MAGNANIMO. S. D

AGNVS Cosmus Magnanime Iuliae auus tuus patro
nus saepe platonicu illud habebat in ore: nihil ad aegregi
as res agendas accomodatius ee q prudentiu doctoruq;
uiroru beniuolentia: Nulluq; certius argumetu esse uel
iustitie prudetieq; q si amici huiusmoi adsint: uel iniusti
tie & iprudentie q si desint. Aureu hoc Platonis nostri p-
ceptu. Cosmus re ipsa et multomagis q uerbis in oi eius
uita ,pbauit uir certe pcaeteris diues pecuniaru . Longe
ditior hoium: prudetie iustitieq; ditissimus. Atq; id qd ra
rissimu & mirabile e filiu & nepotes huius ois thesauri re
liqt heredes. Quo sit ut in Iuliano meo sene illu ex quo unico post deu salus mea
pendebat agnosca. Nemo est igit que magis saluere cupia q Iulianu. Atq; id qde
quottidie deu precor & obsecro. Vt aut tibi animi mei uotu affectumq; certius de
clarare: uolumen primum epsarum ad amicos mearu tibi amicorum regi dedicare
decreui. Quo & amici omnes ad unum praecipuum referantur amicum: & tu i iis
legendis: quotiens salutem legis: totiens Iulianum a Marsilio itelligas salutari.
De foelicitatis desiderio.

Cosmus Medices Marsilio Ficino Platonico : S.D.

Ontuii heri me in agru charegium: no agri sed ai coledi gratia : Veni ad
nos Marsili qprimu. Fer tecu Platonisnostri libru de sumo bono Que
te isthic arbitror ia e graeca lingua i latina ut pmiseras transtulisse. Nihil
enim ardentius cupio: q quae uia commodius ad foelicitatem ducat cognoscere.
Vale & ueni non absque orphica lyra.

Quae sit ad foelicitatem uia.

Marsilius Ficinus Magno Cosmo. S.D.

Enia ad te cu primum potero q libetissime . Q uid. 'n. gratius q in chare
gio hoc e gratiaru agro una cu cosmo gratiaru patre uersari. Interi accipe
paucis q apud Platonicos uia sit ad foelicitate accomodatissima . Et quis
existime non opportere ci uia mostrari qui ,ppe ia puenit ad calce: desiderio tame
tuo & iabsentia & in psentia obsequendu ee censui: Omnes hoies bene agere hoc
est bene uiuere uolut. Bene aute uiuent si bona illis adsint q plurima . Bona uero
haec dicue. Diuitiae: sanitas: forma: robur: nobilitas generis: honores potetia: pru
dentia: pterea iustitia: fortitudo: teperantia: & pcaeteris oibus sapientia: quae qde
uim oem foelicitatis coplectie. Felicitas quippe in ,pspera optati sinis cosecutione
consistit. Id aute in singulis facultatibus sapietia praebet . Siquide piti tibicines qc
qd tibiarum usus reqrit optime cosecune. Et eruditi gramatici qd ad litteras tum
legendas tu scribendas ptinet. Sapietes quoq; gubernatoresd ,psperum nauigatio
nis portu pcaeteris assecunt. Necno belli dux sapiens qd ad militia atcinet tutius
expedit. Et sapies medicus melius adoptata pducit corporisualitudine. Q uao

Müller: *Deutsche Kalender*

Venice: Ratdolt & Maler, 1478

$6\frac{1}{4}'' \times 5\frac{7}{8}''$

Appianus: *Historia Romana*

Venice: Ratdolt, 1477

$9\frac{1}{2}'' \times 6\frac{3}{4}''$

ita iocundis aliquot sumptis comitibus ,
qui nos perductarent ,confesso equo Mes
sanam reliquimus:sed iter facientibus no
bis Taurominium usque memorabile
nihil comspectum est:summa enim litto
ra eraduntur. A leua statim Rhegium,et
Brutii agri paruo primum ,mox latiori
maris interuallo aperientibus se se paula
tim angustiis prospectantur: a dextra col
les continui imminent, Bacchi tota fera-
cissima plaga , et Mamertinis uinetis mi
nus fortasse , q̃ olim fuit , tanq̃ ab ipsa
uetustate contritis iam laudibus ; sed ta
men satis nunc etiam percelebris. In me
dio ferè itineris, uel paulo amplius castel
lum Nisus ex aeria montis rupe uiatori
bus late prospicitur ; unde illud deue -
ctum.Ouidianum,
Nisiades matres , sicelidésq; nurus.
Incolae uallem etiam omnem, quae sub-
est ,Nisi regionem uocant. B. P. Erit
isto sane modo etiam aliquid infra Tau

P. Bembo: *De Aetna*

Venice: Aldus Manutius, 1495

5″ × 3″

POLIPHILO INCOMINCIA ILSECONDO LIBRO DI
LA SVA HYPNER OTOMACHIA.NEL QVALE PO⹂
LIA ET LVI DISER T ABONDI,IN QVALE MODO ET
VARIO CASO NARRANO INTER CALARIAMEN-
TE IL SVO INAMORAMENTO.

NARRA QVIVI LA DIVA POLIA LA NOBILE ET
ANTIQVA ORIGINE SVA.ET COMO PER LI PREDE
CESSORI SVITRIVISIO FVE EDIFICATO.ET DI QVEL
LA GENTE LELIA ORIVNDA. ET PER QVALE MO⹂
DO DISA VEDVTA ET INSCIA DISCONCIAMENTE
SE INAMOROE DI LEI IL SVO DILECTO POLIPHILO.

E MIE DEBILE VOCE TALE O GRA
tiose & diue Nymphe absone peruenerâno &
inconcine alla uostra benigna audiétia , quale
laterrifica raucitate del urinante Esacho al sua⹂
ue canto dela piangeuole Philomela. Nondi
meno uolendo io cum tuti gli mei exili cona⹂
ti del intellecto,& cum la mia paucula sufficié
tia di satisfare alle uostre piaceuole petitone,
non ristaro al potere.Lequale semota qualúque hesitatione epse piu che
si congruerebbe altronde,dignamente meritano piu uberrimo fluuio di
eloqouentia,cum troppo piu rotunda elegantia& cum piu exornata poli
tura di pronútiato,che in me per alcuno pacto non si troua, di cóseguire
il suo gratio so affecto. Ma a uui Celibe Nymphe & adme alquáto,quan
túche & confusa & incomptaméte fringultiéte haro in qualche portiun⹂
cúla gratificato assai.Quando uoluntarosa & diuota a gli desii uostri &
postulato me prestaro piu presto cum lanimo nó mediocre prompto hu⹂
mile parendo,che cum enucleata tersa,&uenusta eloquentia placédo.La
prisca dunque& ueterrima geneologia,& prosapia,& il fatale mio amore
garrulando ordire.Onde gia essendo nel uostro uenerando conuentuale
conspecto,& uederme sterile& ieiuna di eloquio& ad tanto prestáte & di
uo ceto di uui O Nymphe sedule samularie dil acceso cupidine.Et itan⹂
to benigno & delecteuole & sacro sito,di sincere aure & florigeri spirami⹂
ni afflato.Io acconciamente compulsa di assumere uno uenerabile auso,
& tranquillo timore de dire. Dunque auante il tuto uenia date,o bellissi⹂
me & beatissime Nymphe a questo mio blacterare & agli semelli & terri⹂
geni,& pusilluli Conati,si aduene che in alchuna parte io incautamente

A

Poliphilus: *Hypnerotomachia*

Venice: Aldus Manutius, 1499

$8\frac{3}{4}'' \times 5\frac{1}{4}''$

TRIVMPHVS

ce ligatura alla fistula tubale, Gli altri dui cū ueterrimi cornitibici con-
cordi ciascuno & cum gli instrumenti delle Equitante nymphe.
   Sotto lequale triūphale seiughe era laxide nel meditullo, Nelq̇le gli
rotali radii erano infrxi, deliniamento Balustico, gracilifcenti seposa
negli mucronati labijcūm uno pomulo alla circunferentia. Elquale
Polo era di finiffimo & ponderofo oro, repudiante el rodicabile erugi-
ne, & lo'incēdiofo Vulcano, della uirtute & pace exitiale ueneno. Sum-
mamente dagli festigianti celebrato, cum moderate, & repentine
riuolutiōe intorno saltanti, cum solemniffimi plausi, cum
gli habiti cincti di fasceole uolitante, Et le sedente sopra gli trahenti centauri. La Sancta cagione,
& diuino mysterio, inuoce cōsone & car-
mini cancionali cum extre
ma exultatione amo-
rosamente lauda
uano.
** 
*

Poliphilus: *Hypnerotomachia*

Venice: Aldus Manutius, 1499

$8\frac{3}{8}'' \times 5\frac{1}{8}''$

to humilmente.    Epiſtola .xv.

Vanto deſiderio & uo-
lunta ho io de eſſere ho
ra preſente al uoſtro cō
uento & abraciare con
letitia tutto el maraui-
glioſo uoſtro coſortio.
Bene che queſti ochi nō lo meritino. Io
riſguardarei el diſerto piu dlecteuole.che
tutte le cita. Io uederei li, luochi deſerti.
de habitatori.eſſere occupati dale compa
gnie deli ſancti. ad modo duno paradiſo. Ma pche qſto hanno facto li mei pec
cati che el mio capo repieno de ogni ui-
tio nō ſe meſcoli nela cōpagnia deli bea
ti. perho priego uui liqli io nō dubito che
nō poſſiate ipetrare che con le uoſtre ora
tiōe me liberati dale tenebre dī queſto ſe
culo. Et gia ue lhaueua dicto:quando io e-
ra preſente: & hora per littere nō ceſſo di
manifeſtarui el mio deſiderio.che la mia
mēte e adcio rapta con ogni cupidita:ho
ra ſe aptiene a uui che lo effecto ſeguiti la
uolunta. A me ſe apertiene di uolere:& a
le uoſtre oratōe che io uoglia.& poſſi.Io
ſonto come una morboſa pecorella.ſma
rita da tutta la grege. Et ſe el buono pa-
ſtore poſto me ſu le ſue ſpale.nō mi ripor
ta ala ſtalla le forze mi mācharano in ca
mino:Et mēte che io mi ſforzaro di rele
uarmi mi caſcharāno le gābe.Io ſonto ql
lo prodigo figliuolo elquale diſſipata
tutta la ſubſtātia.laqle el padre me haue
ua data nō mi ſono anchora ingenochia-
to a piedi del mio padre.ne ancora ho co
minciato ad caciare uia da me le luſinge
dela luxuria.Et pche uno pocheto nō ſo
lamēte ho cominciato a ſpicarmi da uitii

quāto ancora ho cominciato a uolere nō
hauerli.Hora el diauolo mi lega cō nuoue rete.Hora ppronēdomi nuoui ipedimē
ti.li mari da ogni parte mi circūdano & il
pōto.Hora poſto in mezo delaqua nō uo
glio idrieto tornare.& andare innāci non
poſſo.Reſta che cō la uoſtra oratione lau
ra del ſancto ſpirito me acompagni & ri
duca al porto del deſiderato litto.

Diuo Hieronymo a Paulo uecchio dela
concordia.~    Epiſtola .xvi.

A breuita dl lhumana ui
ta e dānatiōe de peccati
& ſpeſſe uolte nel me-
deſimo naſcimēto dela
luce.ſeguitādo la mor-
te chi naſce.coſeſſa che
ogni dī li ſeculi trāſcorreno neli uitii: per
che quādo el ſerpēte hebe tirato ala terra
el primo habitatore del paradiſo iuilupa
to da nodi uiperini la eternita dela morta
lita mutata.haueua prolūgata la miſeria
del maledecto huomō in noue cēto anni
& piu.Come una tale ſecūda imortalita.
Di poi a poco a poco icrudelēdo el pec-
cato.la ipieta de gigāti aduſſe el periculo
di tutto el mūdo.dapoi qllo bapteſimo
del purgato mūdo:p modo di dire la uita
de gli huomini e abreuiata i picolo tēpo
& ancora queſto breuiſſimo ſpatio habia
mo qſi pduto.ſempre cōbattēdo cō le no
ſtre ſceleritate cōtra ale diuie coſe.Et quā
te uolte ſe uede puenire alcuno ala eta de
cēto anni:o ſe pur ui puiene che nō ſi pen
ta eſſerli puenuto: ſecūdo che teſtifica la
ſcriptura nel libro de pſalmi dicēdo. Edi
dela uita noſtra ſeptāta anni. & ſe ſerāno
piu.ſerāno ottanta.Et cio che piu . e fati

c iii

S. Hiëronymus: *Epistole*

Ferrara: L. de Rossa, 1495

$10\frac{1}{8}'' \times 6\frac{1}{4}''$

IOANNES STELLA SACERDOS VE
NETVS CLARISSIMO SENATORI
ALOVISIO TRIVISANO.S.P.D.

OGITANTI mihi Iam
pridem:cui nam potissimū
Augustalem libellū meum
quē de impatoribus omni
bus cōscripserā essem dica
turus:Vnus in primis oc/
curristi:cuius nomini eū qualiscūq; eēt:quo
tutius uulgaretur destinarē:neq; enim absq;
patrocinio in publicum prodire debuit liber
qui mereri ęternitatē uellet.Stilus est(ut fa/
tear)quo uel itra me possim erubescere.Cæte
rum materies operisq; totius argumentū(ut
arbitror) nō improbabit.Impatoꝝ nomina
uelut breuiario quodā perstricta:claraq; eoꝝ
gesta ediscere cupienti:hec enim.Vtraq; dili
genter collegimus:& quo minus tibi libroꝝ
multoꝝ reuolutione laborandū esset in ordi/
nem certum redegimus:Boni igitur cōsule:
nec q; offerimus magis q̄ tibi deditissimum
offeremus animum inspecta:Vale.

A ii

J. Stella: *Vitae Imperatorum Romanorum*

Venice: De Vitalibus, 1503

$5\frac{1}{2}'' \times 3\frac{1}{4}''$

RIMVS igitur qui Ro/
manū arripuit Imperium
fuit Iulius Cæfar: Lutii fi/ **Primus**
lius ualétiffimus omnium **Ro.Imp.**
principum: qui in uigore
animi non habuit parem
nec ante fe: nec poft fe: hic uixit annis quin/
quaginta fex. Imperauit autem poft finē bel/
lorum fuorum tribus annis & feptem men/
fibus: Interfeƈtus in medio Senatus: uiginti
tribus uulneribus.

CAESAR Auguftus: diƈtus Oƈtauianus a **.XLII.**
natiuitate: pro nepos Cæfaris|& filius ado/ **Imp.Cæ.**
ptiuus fucceffit illi in Impio. Hic fuit feliciffi **Aug.āno**
mus omnium prioꝝ & pofterioru̅: Ṇam alta **X̄p̄s na/**
prouidentia fua imperauit prudenter & lau/ **fcitur.**
dabiliter tot ānis: quot Cæfar uixerat. f. quin
quaginta fex: de quibus regnauit Ɖuodecim
cum Antonio & lepido trium uirorum. Reli
quū tpis folus cū magna pace|& trāquilitate
orbis. Ꝑlaufo tēplo Ianii|& uixit annis feptua
ginta fex minus: triginta quinꝗ diebus: mor
tuus eft feliciter apud Nolā ciuitaté cāpanie.

J. Stella: *Vitae Imperatorum Romanorum*
Venice: De Vitalibus, 1503
$5\frac{3}{8}'' \times 4\frac{1}{8}''$

.i.

EPISTOLE Vtile & deuote de la Beata e Seraphica Vergine Sancta
Catharina da Siena del Sancto ordine de la penitentia de Sancto Dome
nico sposa singulare del saluatore nostro Iesu Christo : le quale lei scri
uea a Summi Pontifici . Cardinali. Archiuescoui . Preti. Frati . Mona
chi. Heremiti. Ad Sore. Mónache. & altre persone deuote: & religiose de
ogni conditione. Item ad R i . Duchi. Conti. Capitani de genti darme:
& altri signori diuersi. Ad Communitati. Regimenti. Ad Doctori. Ca
ualeri: & altre persone diuerse. Seculari. donne de ogni conditione có
fortando quelli che perseuerasseno nel amore del dolce Iesu Crocifixo.
animandoli alle sancte uirtute: & fugere li uitii.

Al nome di Iesu Christo Crocifixo: & di Maria dolce. Al nostro si
gnore lo Papa Gregorio undecimo.　　　　Epistola Prima.

ANCTIssimo & reuerédissimo patre mio in
Christo dolce Iesu. Io Catharina idegna & mi
serabile uťa figliola : serua & schiaua di serui di
Iesu Christo: scriuo a uoi nel ptioso sangue suo
có desiderio de uiderui pastore bono. Conside
rando io patre mio dolce: che il lupo ne porta
le pecorelle uostre: & non si troua chi li remedi
sca: ricorro dunque a uoi patre & pastore no
stro pregandoui da parte di Christo Crocifixo:
che uoi impariate dalui : el quale con tanto foco damore se die all obpro
briosa morte della sanctissima croce: per trare la pecorella smarrita del hu
mana generatione dele mani deli demonii. pero che per la rebelliőe: che
lhomo fece a Dio la posseduano per sua possessione . Viene dunque
la infinita bonta de dio: & uede el male: la damnatione & la ruina di que
sta pecorella : & uede che con ira & con guerra non nela puo trare. Vn
de non stante che sia ingiuriato da essa : pero che per la rebellione: che
lhomo fece: dissobediendo a Dio : meritaua pena infinita . La summa
& eterna sapientia non uole fare cosi: ma troua uno modo piaceuole &
piu dolce & amoroso: che trouare possa: po che uede: che per niuno mo
do si trae il cuore del homo: quanto per amore. pero che le sacto damo
re : & questa pare la cagione che tanto ama: per che nó e sacto daltro: che
damore & primo la nima: & secondo el corpo. pero che per amore Dio el
creo alla imagine & similitudine sua: & per amore la matre gli die della
sua substantia concependo & generando el figliolo: et pero uede do dio
che le tanto apto ad amare: dritamente gitto lhamo dell amore donádoci
el uerbo del unigenito figliolo prendendo la nostra humanita per fare

a

S. Catharina de Siena: *Epistole*

Venice: Aldus Manutius, 1500

$8\frac{3}{4}'' \times 5\frac{1}{8}''$

Marcus Vigerius: *Decachordum Christianum*

Fano: Hier. Soncinus, 1507

$10\frac{1}{8}'' \times 6\frac{5}{8}''$

Considerando io Ioanni Antonio Taiente quanto e ne
ceßaria cosa a li noſtri magnifici gētilhomeni & adaltri
mercatanti ellaudabile modo de tenere conto de li
bro dopio cioe, el zornale, el ſibro con ſalpha-
betto ſecondo el conſueto de queſta incli
ta Citta di Venetia, io qui ſeguendo
con ſagiuto del mio Carißimo
compagno maeſtro Aluiſe
daſa Fontana, ui da
remo ſo amae-
ſtramēto
che con facilita ſo potrete imparare, ſagual opera
ancor ſara di molta utilita Vniuerſal-
mente ad ogniuno, come ne
ſopera uedereti.

G. A. Tagliente: *Modo de tenere conto de libro*

Venice: Tagliente, 1525

$4\frac{5}{8}'' \times 3\frac{7}{8}''$

*Il Petrarca spirituale*

Venice: Marcolini, 1536

$5\frac{5}{8}'' \times 3\frac{3}{4}''$

# CANZONI PREDETTE DI MESSER FRANCESCO PE, TRARCHA DIVENVTO THEOLOGO ET SPIRITVALE.

## CANZONE PRIMA.

*A sciare il uero ben per la falsa ombra*
*Saggio mai non uid'io:*
*Però chi sa, seguendo il buon desio,*
*Ogni altra uoglia del suo core isgom,*

*Quanti pensieri porta l'huom celati,* (bra,
*Ch'hanno la mente desiando morta,*
*Il mondo ha di pieta depinto il uolto,*
*Per ingannar ogni alma poco accorta;*
*Perche son l'opre sue Serpi uelati,*

*Onde, poi ch'in me stesso i son raccolto,*
*Hauendomi il Signor per gratia tolto*
*Dinanzi a gli occhi il uelo;*
*Lodar uo solo lui al caldo e al gelo*
*Per fin che'l corpo oscur lo spirto adombra,*

## CANZONE II.

*Occhi miei lassi; mentre ch'io ui giro*
*Al pio IESV; ch'ha in croce i spirti morti;*
*Pregoui, siate accorti*
*D'accompagnar con pianto il mio sospiro,*
*A lui solo riuolgo i miei pensieri;*
*Lo qual a buon camin l'alma conduce:*

BB ij

*Il Petrarca spirituale*
Venice: Marcolini, 1536
$6\frac{5}{8}'' \times 3\frac{1}{8}''$

IL PROLOGO, SOPRA
LA ZVCCA DEL
DONI.

Al nobiliſſimo Signor Rocco Granza,
ſuo Compare; & maggiore honorando.

In vn paeſe doue ſi tira di baleſtra d a bolzoni molto aſſe-
gnatamente ; dice che fu vn tratto vn aſtuto bale-
ſtrieri , ilqual tirando a mira per dar nel capo a vn'altro , non gli venne colto , per buona ventura . Colui
vedutoſi volare il bolzone coſi apreſſo alle tempie , &
tanto accoſto che raſentandolo gli fece vento , ſi comin-
ciò a conturbar tutto . Onde il traditore voltandola in
ridere diſſe , haueſti paura ſocio? da queſto ſaluto da ca-
ni ſi leuo vn prouerbio ; ſe coglie colga , ſe non , haueſti
paura? Vo dir coſi , che io ho dato della mia Zucca ſul
capo a parecchi pazzeroni e buon anno. Ma ſe per ſorte
nel dar giu la ramatata , la mia Zucca ſia piena di ſa-
le , di ſemi , di ciuaie , o d'altra coſa laqual ſia peſante;
io credo che la darà loro vn mal crocchio , & ſe per
mala diſgratia la troua ſola la buca , ( che'l granchio fuſ-
ſe ito a ſpaſſo ) la farà maggiore ſcoppio , & rintrone-
ra piu loro il capo . Vltimamente ſe la s'abatte ad ac-
chiappare ſcoperta la Zucca ; i poueri capaßoni hanno fat
to il pane : percioche la ne darà loro vna ſi fatta che'l
muro gne ne darà vn'altra ; hor ſia con Dio .
Vn'altro auuerbio ſalta in campo ilqual è cauato da dotti
in lettera , cioè ; ogni ritto ha il ſuo roueſcio , ideſt ,
ſe la mia Zucca ſia piena di vento come le palle ; di bor
ra come i zimbelli , o di capecchio come i carelli ; o col-

A ii

A. F. Doni: *La Zucca*

Venice: Marcolini, 1551

$5\frac{1}{4}'' \times 3''$

ƐPISTOLA DEL TRISSINO
DE LE LETTERE
NꞶƱωVAMENTE AGGIVNTE
NE LA LINGꞶA
ITALIANA.

Con Grazia ε Prohibizione del Sommo Pontefice, ε del Senato
Veneto, che nessuno possa ſtampare que ſta opera.

G. G. Trissino: *De le lettere*

Vicenza: Janiculo, 1529

$6\frac{7}{8}'' \times 3\frac{1}{2}''$

## PTOLOMEO IANICVLO A LI LETTORI.

La bontà et utilità de le cose, ω Lettori, suole essere sempre speciale cagione, che esse siano da gli homini amate, et accettate; et se pur qualche maligna, et invidiosa nebbia tal hora tanto le cuopre, che siano da le genti biasimate, e rifiutate, adviene poi, che quando da la ragione, ω dal tempo vengono scoperte, subito sono disiate, et abbracciate. La onde vedendo io di quanta utilità, anzi necessità siano a la scrittura Italiana le lettere ritrovate dal Trissino, di maniera, che non è possibile senza esse ad imparare a leggere, ne Cortigiano, ne Toscano, ne niuna de l'altre belle lingue d'Italia a chi non le sa, ne a chi le sa poter senza esse drittamente scriverle, ne ad altri propriamente manifestarle, ho voluto un'altra volta stampare la Epistola, che egli di esse lettere scrisse a Papa Clemente Settimo, che di presente è Sommo Pontefice, acciò, che questa nostra lingua si possa fin da i primi elementi imparare, et ampliare. Ma perche alcini (da che cagione sospinti non sò) hanno piu audacemente, che dottamente contra si biasima, si utile, e si admiranda invenzione scritto, e con la invidiosa nebula de la loro eloquenzia hanno quasi adombrato la incredibile utilità di essa; Però vedendo io tale utilità di tempo in tempo maggiormente scoprirsi, e tanto piu necessaria parere, quanto, che ogni giorno questa lingua piu s'abbellisse, e di dotte, e dilettevoli composizioni si fa piu ricca, mi son messo per commune utilità a ristampare (come ho detto) la predetta Epistola, la quale in qualche particella è stata da esso Autore fatta piu lucida, e piu chiara. Ma conciò sia, che egli non habbia mai voluto rispondere a coloro, che gli hanno scritto contra, Dicendo, che nel loro indotto scrivere essi medesmi contradicendosi appresso i dotti si rispondeno, appresso gli imperiti poi saribbe cosa superflua il multiplicar in parole. E se pur qualcuno si vorrà di tal dubbio meglio chiarire, legga i scritti di M. Vicenzo Oreadino da Perugia, il quale di queste lettere dottissimamente ragiona, et a i riprensori di esse prudentissimamente risponde, et ivi troverà, che non senza necessarie, e validissime ragioni sono state ritrovate, et mandate in luce. Purio (poi che'l Trissino non ha voluto in ciò altrimenti rescrivere) aggiungerò ad essa Epistola alcune cosette tratte da i dubbii grammaticali di esso Trissino, et alcune altre tradotte da la predetta copera latina de l'Oreadino, acciò che le menti de i studiosi di questa lingua possano essere circa tali lettere piu illuminate, e chiare.

G. G. Trissino: *De le lettere*

Vicenza: Janiculo, 1529

$8\frac{1}{8}'' \times 4\frac{1}{2}''$

152

## L. COELII LACTANTII FIRMIANI DIVINARVM INSTITVTIONVM, ADVERSVS GENTEIS, LIBER QVINTVS, DE IVSTITIA AD CONSTANTINVM IMPERATOREM.

On est apud me dubium, Constantine Imperator Max. quin hoc
n opus nostrum, quo singularis ille
rerum conditor, & huius immen-
si rector asseritur, siquis attigerit
ex istis inepte religiosis (ut sunt ni=
mia superstitione impatientes) insectitur etiam male-
dictis, & uix lecto fortasse principio, affligat, proij=
ciat, execretur; seq́; inexpiabili scelere contaminari,
atque astringi putet, si hæc aut legat patienter, aut
audiat. Ab hoc tamen, si fieri potest, humanitatis iure postulamus, ut non prius damnet, quàm uniuersa
cognouerit. nam si sacrilegis, & proditoribus, & ue-
neficis potestas defendendi sui datur; nec prædam-
nari quenq̃ incognita causa licet: non iniuste petere
uidemur, ut siquis erit ille, qui inciderit in hæc; si le-
get, perlegat; si audiet, sententiam differat in extre-
mum. sed noui hominum pertinaciam; nunq̃ impetra-
bimus. Timent enim ne à nobis reuicti, manus dare
aliquando, clamante ipsa ueritate cogantur. Obstre-
punt igitur, & intercedunt, ne audiant; & oculos suos

Lactantius

Venice: Aldi heredes, 1535

$4\frac{3}{4}'' \times 2\frac{1}{2}''$

# QVIVI COMINCIA LA SECONDA PARTE CHE APPARTIENE AL VIAGGIO CHE IO IOSA= PHAT BARBARO FECI IN PERSIA COME AMBASCIA= TORE.

SSENDO la nostra Illustrissima Signoria in guerra con l'Ottomano del. 1471. Io come huomo uso à stien= tar, & prattico tra gente Barbara, & uolonteroso di tutto il bene di essa Illu= strissima Signoria, fui mandato insieme con uno Amba= sciator de Assambei signor della Persia, ilqual era uenu= to à Venetia à confortar la Illustrissima Signoria che uo lesse proseguir la guerra contra il detto Ottomano; con ciosiache ancora lui con le sue forze gli uen'u à incontra. Partimmo adunque da Venetia con due galee sottili & drieto di noi uennero due galee grosse cariche di artiglie rie, & gente da fatti, & presenti che mandaua detta Illustrissima Signoria al detto Assambei, con commissio= ne che io mi appresentassi al paese del Caramano, & a' quelle marine; & uenendo ouer mandando li Assambei gli donassi tutte dette cose. Le arteglierie furono bom= barde, spingarde, schioppetti, poluere da tirare, carri et ferraméti di diuerse sorti nella ualuta de ducati quatro= mila. Le genti da fatti, furono balestrieri, & schiopet=

*Viaggi fatti alla Tana*

Venice: Aldi filii, 1545

$5'' \times 2\frac{1}{2}''$

SCIPIONIS CAPICII
DE PRINCIPIIS RERVM
LIBRI DVO.

EIVSDEM
DE VATE MAXIMO
LIBRI TRES.

ALDI FILII

VENETIIS, M. D. XLVI.

Scipio Capicius: *De Principiis Rerum*
Venice: Aldi filii, 1546
$4\frac{1}{2}'' \times 2\frac{3}{8}''$

# ELOGIA VERIS CLA,
## RORVM VIRORVM IMAGINIBVS
### APPOSITA.

## QVÆ IN MVSÆO IOVIANO
## COMI SPECTANTVR.

*ADDITA IN CALCE OPERIS*
*ADRIANI PONT. VITA.*

*Ne turbata uolent rapidis oracula uentis*

*Nunc folio uates commodiore fonat.*

SYBILLA

Cum priuilegio ſummi Pontificis, Caroli V . Imperat . Regis Franciæ.
Illuſtriſſimi Senatus Veneti , nec non Excellentiſſimorum
Florentiæ , & Mantuæ Ducum .

P. Giovio: *Elogia Veris Clarorum Virorum Imaginibus Apposita*

Venice: Tramezzino, 1546

$8\frac{1}{4}'' \times 5\frac{1}{4}''$

DELLA GVERRA

# DI CAMPAGNA
## DI ROMA,

ET DEL REGNO DI NAPOLI,

NEL PONTIFICATO DI PAOLO IIII.

L'ANNO M. D. LVI. ET LVII,

TRE RAGIONAMENTI DEL SIGNOR
ALESSANDRO ANDREA,

Nuouamente mandati in luce

DA GIROLAMO RVSCELLI.

CON PRIVILEGII.

IN VENETIA,

Per Gio. Andrea Valuaſſori. M. D. LX.

Ruscelli: *Della guerra di Campagna di Roma*

Venice: Vavassore, 1560

6″ × 4″

ALLO ILLVSTRISS. E REVE-

RENDISS. MONSIGNORE IL S. ANTO-

NIO PERINOTO, VESCOVO DI ARRA'S

E PRIMO DEL CONSIGLIO

DI CESARE.

 GLI non m'è afcofo, Illuftriß.e Reue-
rendiß.Signore, che molti non fenza ca
gione, fi marauiglieranno, che io a gui-
fa di poco prudente iftimator della qua-
lità delle cofe,e della debolezza delle mie
forze, mi fia lafciato trafcorrere tanto
auanti, che habbia prefo ardire di de-
dicar la prefente opera non pure a uno Imperadore(cofa, che
da per fe douerebbe fpauentar ciafcuno alto ingegno)ma al mag
giore Imperadore, che dalla età del primo CESARE a quefti
tempi, fia per tanti fecoli ftato degno d'hauere ottenuto il mondo: et) oltre a cio mi fia afsicurato ancora d'entrar nel campo
delle fue laudi.Percioche chi non fa, che al ualor fopra humano,
et) alla prodezza incomparabile di CARLO QVINTO,
fi ricerca folamente la chiara tromba del gran Virgilio, o del
Diuino Homero? e con tutto cio non fono baftanti gl'inchio-
ftri per celebrarle: ne conuiene, che ogni rozo ingegno ardifca

* ij

Ludovico Dolce: *Le Trasformationi*
Venice: Giolito, 1553
7″ × 4″

## CAVSA DI SOSPIRI
### PALLORE ET LAGRIME
### D'AMANTI.

**D**VE sono, tra le altre, principali parti del corpo humano, cerebro et cuore: in uno è la seggia della sapientia: nell'altro della vita. Et benche cosi siano congionti, che l'uno all'altro senza intermissione si porgan sempre aiuto, pure uedemo manifestamente, il cerebro piu dell'animo, il cuor piu del corpo participare: & questo piu circa le mēbra, quello piu con l'intelletto dominare: quantunque il cerebro fare il tutto creda Platone: Galeno fonte delle uene istima lo segato: Aristotele & Auicenna fonte del sangue cresero il cuore: in questo poneno la mestitia. Noi cō Christiani nostri tenemo il cuore esser fonte di uita, membro delli altri principe, che se Varrone diffini l'anima essere aere temperato nel cuore, se Empedocle disse l'anima esser sangue che sta intorno al cuore, se Plinio crese nel cuor esser la mente, se a Cicerone par che'l cuore sia l'animo se Aristotele lo fa capo di sensi, chi dubita da costui ogni nostra passione amorosa prouenire? Tra l'altre membra principali dunque credemo il cuore sentire la sollecitudine: essendo in angustia tiramo il spirito dal intimo petto, donde sospiro si chiama, argomento, & indicio d'esser stato in pensieri. Ilche quando accade si eleua il pulmone: per laqual cosa sospirato è uno morbo che procede da lui: dellaquale infermità non solamente li Phisici, ma Ouidio fa mentione. Et chi in tal

M  v

Marco Equicola: *Libro di Natura d'Amore*

Venice: Giolito, 1554

$4\frac{5}{8}'' \times 2\frac{1}{4}''$

# IL DECAMERONE

## DI M. GIOVANNI BOC=

CACCIO EMENDATO SE
condo gli antichi essemplari, per
giudicio & diligenza di
piu autori,

## DI NVOVO RISTAMPATO

& con somma diligenza & studio corretto, & in piu
luoghi reuisto.

### CON PRIVILEGIO.

IN VINEGIA APPRESSO GABRIEL
GIOLITO DE FERRARI
M D L.

Boccaccio: *Il Decamerone*

Venice: Giolito, 1550

$4\frac{3}{8}'' \times 2\frac{1}{4}''$

⁋Epiſtola di Frate Hieronymo da Fertara
dellordine de frati predicatori a uno Amico.

DIlectiſſimo in
Chriſto Ieſu.
Io miſono aſſai
marauigliato che perle
cōtradictioni delli huo
mini puerſi & calūnie a
me date/tu ſia alquāto
debilitato nella uia del
la uerita/come ſe tu nō
ſapeſſi nō eſſer coſa nuo
ua/che lauerita euāgeli
ca ſempre habbi hauu
ta grande contradictio
ne: pche eſſendo q̄ſta ſo
la cb conduce alla ſalu
te/loaduerſario di Xp̄o
Sathanas bencb ſia ini
mico dogni uerita/nientedimeno contra queſta euange
lica concita tutto elmōdo/inſtigato dalla inuidia: pche
nō uorrebbe che lhuomo acquiſtaſſi quella gloria/della
quale lui perla ſua ſuperbia e ſtato priuato. Et pero lui
non perſeguita lauerita della philoſophia/ne alcuna al
tra uerita: pche ſēza laſede ſono di poca utilita. Riuol
gi lehiſtorie del uecchio & del nuouo teſtamento/& tro
uerrai molte maggiori cōtradictioni eſſer ſtate nelli tē
pi paſſati cōtra lauerita/laquale conduce alla ſalute &
contro alli ſuoi predicatori/che nō e nel tēpo preſēte.
Et benche ogni huomo che mha udito/ſia/o poſſa eſſer
certo che lecalūnie che miſono date/ſono manifeſtamē
te falſe/ & parte ancora i ſcripto lho dimoſtrato: Nien
tedimeno eſſendo tu abſente/& udendo ogni giorno di
re molti mali ſenza alchuna c efenſione della uerita/ſo
no excitato dalla charita laquale io tiporto/in q̄ſta let
tera defendere lauerita/& dimoſtrarti quanto ſono fri
uole lecalūnie delli noſtri aduerſarii. ⁋Imprimis alcu
ni dicono che io ſono heretico/& parlano con poca pru

a i

Savonarola: *Epistola*

Florence: s.a. et l. (Proctor, 6396)

$6\frac{3}{8}'' \times 3\frac{3}{4}''$

¶ Prediche utilissime per la quadragesima del re
uerēdo padre frate hieronymo Sauonarola da Fer
rara de lordine de frati predicatori sopra Ezechiel
propheta: & etiam sopra lo sacro Euangelio.

Aperientur labia mea ut recte predicent. Iusti
sunt sermones mei nō est in eis prauitas neqʒ
quid peruersum. Recti sunt intelligentibus &
equi inuenientibus scientiam. Prouerbi. viii.

Savonarola: *Prediche*

Florence: B. Benalio, 1517

$7\frac{1}{2}'' \times 5''$

PAVSANIAE VE
TERIS GRAECIAE
DESCRIPTIO.

Romulus Amasæus vertit.

Accessit rerum in hisce libris
memorabilium locupletis-
simus index.

L. Torrentinus Ducalis Typographus excudebat.
FLORENTIAE.   MDLI.

Pausanias: *Veteris Graeciae descriptio*

Florence: Torrentino, 1551

$11\frac{1}{2}'' \times 6\frac{1}{4}''$

# ROMVLVS ³
## AMASAEVS ALE
### XANDRO FARNESIO
### CARDINALI PAVLI III.
#### PONT. MAX. NEPOTI

##### S. P. D.

VM Sæpe animaduerterim, Ale
xander Farnesi, solere te ab assi-
duis curis, atque occupationibus
quasi respirantem, vel in literato-
rum hominum sermone, & consuetudine, vel in optimorum scri-
ptorum lectione conquiescere, de
variis, ac multis lucubrationibus
meis, latinè iam, ni fallor, mea
opera loquentem Pausaniam, tibi,
cui iam pridem, non magis fortunæ amplitudine, quam
virtutis tuæ adductus excellentia, me ipsum addixi, no
minatim dedendum censui : non quia Græcorum aucto-
rum à puero lectione assuefactus, Græca illum vtentem
lingua non fueris planissimè intellecturus, sed quod omni
no Romani Principis auribus Latinæ orationis sonum
aptiorem, & grauiorem fore existimaui. Atque is quidem
veterem Græciam in libros decem descriptam oculis penè
subiiciens, parem propè tibi voluptatem poterit apportare,
ac ipsa solita est ad exteros Europæ populos suscepta iam
toties peregrinatio : Cum peradolescens, magna cum tua
laude, Hispaniam, Galliam, Germaniam, de maximis
Reip. negociis legatus obiisti. Atque eo tibi erit fortasse
lectio huius historiæ iucundior, quòd quæ semel placue-
rint loca, non ut illa cursim, & festinanter, sed inter quie
scendum, quoties libitum fuerit, licebit reuisere. Neque
verò te magis ( credo ) eas regiones animo lustrantem, in

A

Pausanias: *Veteris Graeciae descriptio*

Florence: Torrentino, 1551

$9\frac{3}{8}'' \times 5''$

G

# ACHILLIS BOCCHII

## BONON. SYMBOLICARVM
### QVAESTIONVM DE VNIVERSO
#### GENERE QVAS SERIO LVDEBAT
#### LIBRI QVINQVE.

CONDICTIO

ATTENDE LECTOR OPTIME,
SI FORTE QVID CONTRA PATRVM
DECRETA SANCTORVM PIA,
FACTVMVE DICTVMVE HIS LIBRIS,
INFECTVM ID, INDICTVMVE SIT.

SACROSANCTA IVLI. III. PON. MAX.
LEGE CAVTVM EST
NE QVIS HOC POEMA AVTORE INSCIO
IN VITOVE DE CAETERO IMPRIMERE
NEVE VENALE HABERE
VSPIAM AVDEAT.

BONONIAE

IN AEDIB. NOVAE ACADEMIAE
BOCCHIANAE.
M. D. LXV.

Achilles Bocchi: *Symbolicae Quaestiones*

Bologna: Bocchi, 1555

$5\frac{1}{4}'' \times 3\frac{5}{8}''$

## LIB. PRIM.

## LECTORI STVDIOSO, ET ELEGANTI.

### SYMB. SYMBOLORVM.

Quid symbolum sit, ne amplius
    Roges, breuiſſime, ut poteſt,
    Conabimur nunc edere.
Eſt nanq; signum ΣΥΜΒΟΛΟΝ
    Vt signa militaria.
    Collatio etiam dicitur,
    Quòd multi in unum conferunt.
Hinc ſymbolum Terentius
    Poeta dixit nobilis.
Orator ARPINAS notam,
    Sed Anulum Graij uocant
    Plærunq; signatorum.
Porrò omen, atq; insignia.
    Iſto quoq; ipſo nomine
    Quædam notantur teſſeræ,
Quæ à ciuitatibus dari
    Solent quibuſdam, publicè
    Vt quenq; par sit accipi,
In fœderatis oppidis,
    Amicè, & hoſpitaliter.
    Sic poſſumus iam teſſeras

Achilles Bocchi: *Symbolicae Quaestiones*

Bologna: Bocchi, 1555

$6'' \times 3\frac{1}{8}''$

# IL
# MORGANTE
## DI LVIGI PVLCI,
### NOBIL' FIORENTINO.

*Nuouamente corretto, e Riſtampato con licenzia.*
*de SVPERIORI.*

CON PRIVILEGIO DEL SERENISSIMO
GRAN DVCA DI TOSCANA.

*IN FIORENZA,*
Nella Stamperia di Bartolomeo Sermartelli.
MDL.XXIIII.

Luigi Pulci: *Il Morgante*

Florence: Sermartelli, 1574

$7\frac{1}{2}'' \times 4\frac{1}{2}''$

72    *C A N T O*

94

Reſtaua à punto il traditor di Gano,
Carlo non volle che gl'vſciſſe fore,
Tornoſſi Mattafolle, a mont'albano,
Preſſo alla terra ou'era il ſuo ſignore,

E preſentò i prigioni al Re pagano,
Herminion fe lor maſſimo honore,
E nel ſuo padiglion gli ha riceuuti,
Chriſto del ciel ci conſerui, e aiuti.

## CANTO NONO

ORlando, Rinaldo & gl'altri ſi partono da Ca
radoro, riſcontrano Fieramonte qual'era re-
ſtato al gouerno d'Herminione, Rinaldo com-
batte ſeco & l'ammazza, pigliono la Città, vcci
dono la moglie è figliuoli d'Erminione, dipoi
caualcono al ſoccorſo di Francia.

I

*FELICE alma d'ogni grazia piena,*
Fida colonna, e ſpeme grazioſa,
Vergine ſacra humile, e nazarena,
Perche tu ſe di Dio nel cielo ſpoſa,
Con la tua man inſin al fin mi mena,
Che di mia fantaſia troui ogni chioſa,
Sol per la tua benignita ch'è molta,
Acciò ch'el mio cantar piaccia a chi aſcolta.

2
Phebo haue a gia nell'oceano il volto,
E bagnaua fra l'onde i ſuoi crin d'auro,
E dal noſtro emiſpero haue a tolto,
Ogni ſpendor laſciando il ſuo bel lauro.

Dal qual fu gia miſeramente ſciolto,
Era nel tempo che piu ſcalda il Tauro,
Quando il Daneſe, e gl'altri al padiglione,
Si ritrouar del grande Herminione,

3
Herminion fe far pel campo feſta,
Paruegli queſto buon cominciamento,
E Mattafolle haue drieto gran geſta,
Di gente armata, a ſuo contentamento,
E'ndoſſo haueu'vna ſua ſopraueſta,
Dou'era vn Macometto in pur'argento,
Tel campo a ſpaſſo con gran feſta andaua,
Di ſua prodezza ognun molto parlaua.

4
E ſi doleua Mattafolle ſolo,
Ch'Aſtolfo vn tratto non venga, a cadere,
E minacciaua in mezzo del ſuo ſtuolo,
E porta vna fenice per cimiere,
Aſtolfo ne ſare venuto a volo,
Per cader vna volta à ſuo piacere,
Ma Ricciardetto che ſapea l'humore,
Non vuol per nulla ch'egli ſbuchi fuore.

*Carlo*

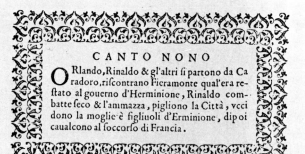

Luigi Pulci: *Il Morgante*

Florence: Sermartelli, 1574

$7\frac{1}{2}'' \times 4\frac{7}{8}''$

ORATIONE DI.M.GIOVAN
GIORGIO TRISSINO
AL SERENISSIMO
M.ANDREA GRITI
PRINCIPE DI VENETIA.

ELLA, ET HONORE=
b vole consuetudine è questa, Sereniss=
simo Principe, et Illustrissima Signo=
ria, che dopo la creatione di ciascun Duce tutte le
città suggette a questo felicissimo stato mandino i
loro ambasciadori a sua Serenità. Il che, oltre che
è segno di obedientia, e di amore, è anchora assai
buona occasione di farsi grate, e di raccomandare
se stesse con questo mezo al Principe nuovo. La
quale consuetudine volendo hora la vostra fede=
lissima città di Vicenza exequire, mi ha, insieme
con questi miei honorati Colleghi, eletto, e man=
dato a Vostra Serenità, et appresso mi ha dato il
carico di fare la oratione; la quale quantunque io
sapesse essere da se difficillima impresa, si per mol=
te altre ragioni, come etiandio per la contrarietà,

A ij

G. G. Trissino: *Oratione*

Rome: Vicentino, 1524

$5\frac{1}{2}'' \times 2\frac{7}{8}''$

Pandulphi Collenucii Iurisconsulti, ad
Illustrisimum Herculem, Ferra-
riensium Ducem Inclytum,
Apologus, cui
Titulus

## A L I T H I A

Raues quondam ALITHIA,
cum VANITATE inimici-
tias exercuerat, et cū magnis utraq̃
uiribus pollere uiderētur, ingentia insuper præ-
mia iis qui alterutram partē sequerentur osten
derent, uniuersum penc orbem (magno gentium
omnium malo) in se conuerterant, Et non pri-
uatos homines modo, sed et ciuitates ipsas, pro-
uintiasq̃, et nationes, partium studia incende-
rant, aliis ALITHIAM, aliis VANI-
TATEM inuocantibus. De genere primũ
contētiones ortæ sunt, utraq̃ in Deos genus re
ferēte, Illa Iouem, Hæc ditem originis auctorē

M 2

Compoſta da l'authore nel . M . D . X X I X .
d'Aprile, & ſtampata poi in Roma da
Antonio Blado Aſolano nel . M . D .
X X X I I I I . di Marzo .

Cl. Tolomei: *Oratione de la pace*

Rome: Blado, 1534

$4\frac{3}{8}'' \times 3\frac{1}{4}''$

VITA SFORTIAE CLARISS.DV,

CIS A PAVLO IOVIO CON,

SCIPTA, AD GVIDONEM

ASCANIVM SFORT. A`

SANCTA FLORA CAR

DIN. AERARIIQVE

PRAEFECTVM.

ROMAE M. D. XXXIX.

P. Giovio: *Vita sfortiae*
Rome: Blado, 1539
$5\frac{1}{2}'' \times 3\frac{5}{8}''$

P. Giovio: *Vita sfortiae*

Rome: Blado, 1539

$4\frac{7}{8}'' \times 3\frac{1}{4}''$

# VITA SFORTIAE CLARISS. DVCIS A` PAVLO IOVIO CONSCRIPTA, AD GVIDONEM ASCANIVM SFORT. A` SANCTA FLORA CARDIN. AERARIIQVE PRAEFECTVM.

q Vum honorem Senatoriæ dignitatis, quem tibi planè adolescenti maternus auus PAVLVS Tertius Pont. Max. insigni iudicio, sed maturius fortasse, quàm speraras, mandauit: cum uirtutis indole, tum claritate familiæ, adeò egregie sustentes, ut maiore fortuna dignus esse uideare : Pergratum omnino futurum existimaui; si tibi ardenti animo uirtutem complectenti, nouæ faces adderentur, ductæ scilicet à maiorum tuorum exemplis, SFORTIAEꝗ præsertim abaui tui; qui summa cum laude amplissimis rebus gestis familiæ uestræ immortale cognomen dedit. Eius enim uiri bello memorabilis dicta, factáque solerti indagatione ex uarijs, ineptisꝗ sæpe rerum scriptoribus excerpta in Enchiridion descripsi, ut ad imaginem tanto frontis honore conspicuam, quam domi pictam assidue contemplaris, excelsi quoque animi similitudo ad ueram effigiem stilo expressa, non indecenter accederet. Itaꝗ enitere GVI-

a ii

P. Giovio: *Vita sfortiae*

Rome: Blado, 1539

$6\frac{1}{2}'' \times 3\frac{5}{8}''$

## PARTE XXXIII

anco profiteuole, & auantaggioso il procedere col detto pie sini
stro, ponendosi con quello innanzi, in Prima Guardia, come ne
la seguente figura, onde secondo il parer' mio, et per le ragioni, le
quali à tal proposito giudico esser migliori, dico che, simili sorti di
Guardie ponno accettarsi in parte, & con le conditioni giustifi-
cate, et neccessarie, che di sotto si diranno, ma non gia, quando cō-
battesse vno co'l nemico, quale fosse di pari forza, et si ritrouas-
sero amendoi in camisa, e'l detto nemico se li presentasse cōtra in
detta Guardia di Prima, co'l pie sinistro innanzi, perche fermā
dosi Questo verso lui in Quarta ordinaria larga, col pie destro
innanzi, subito giunto, li andarebbe incontro firmandosi in Terza stretta, et non mouendosi l'auersario insino à tanto, che Questo ancora fosse arriuato in detta Terza, spingerebbe di Secon-
da sopra il suo pugnale, ciò è de l'auersario, doue volendo alzar-
si la punta con detto pugnale, per mandarla fore con animo di tra
passar' verso lui, verebbe da se à firmarsi la spada ne la persona
la quale ne l'approsimarsi, tanto maggiormente anco si discopri-
rebbe, & offerirebbesi al colpo. Il che se pure occorresse à
Questo, ritrouandosi per caso ne la detta Guardia di Prima, co
me staua l'altro col pie sinistro innanzi, uolgerebbe alquanto in
dentro la spalla sinistra, solamente per schifar il parare, essendo
prohibito per le ragioni gia dette, accompagnando la spada del ne
mico in fore, & passata via se lui saltasse indietro
lo seguitarebbe con la punta d'im-
broccata destra in Quarta
larga, & lunge.

I

Camillo Agrippa: *Trattato di scientia d'arme*

Rome: Blado, 1553

$6\frac{3}{4}'' \times 4\frac{1}{8}''$

# ILLVSTRISS. ET ECCELLENTISS

## DOMINO D. ET PATRONO

### MEO COLENDISSIMO,

## D. M. ANTONIO COLVMNAE, ETC.

## M. ANTONIVS BARDVS

### SENENSIS.

Fœlicitatem.

 VM Antiquiſsimo ROMA-
NORVM tempore ſine cer-
ta lege, ſine certo Iure ROM.
Ciuitas uiuere incepiſſet, ac manu
Principis, & Regis omnia guber-
narentur, auctaque indè Ciuita-
te ad Magiſtratuum diſtinctionem, diuerſis temporibus de
uenire placuit: inter quos tunc, ille pernceeſſarius Aedilium
Curulium Magiſtratus fuit aggregatus. Sed cum idem
(etiam tempore Max. Pontificum) receſſiſſet ab uſu uel inor
dinatè eſſet diſtributus, MARTINVS fœl. record.
huius Nominis Papa Quintus, Doctrina omnique Virtute,
ac Bonitate præditus, ex tua Antiquiſſima Nobiliſsima,
què Columnenſium Familia oriundus, Almam Vrbem de-
corare, & augere cupiens, (ubi CHRISTVS Sedem
Apo-

Ant. Bardus: *Tractatus Iuris*

Rome: Blado, 1565

$6\frac{1}{4}'' \times 3\frac{1}{2}''$

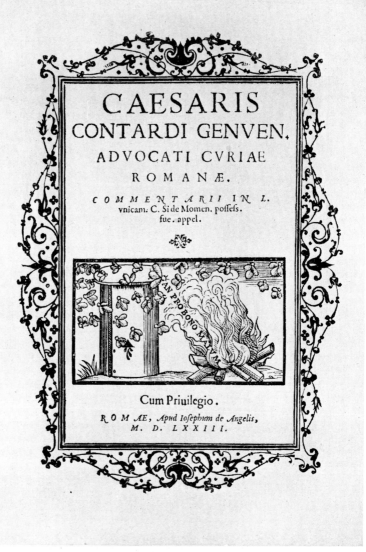

C. Contardi: *Commentarii*

Rome: Joseph de Angelis, 1573

$7\frac{1}{4}'' \times 5\frac{1}{4}''$

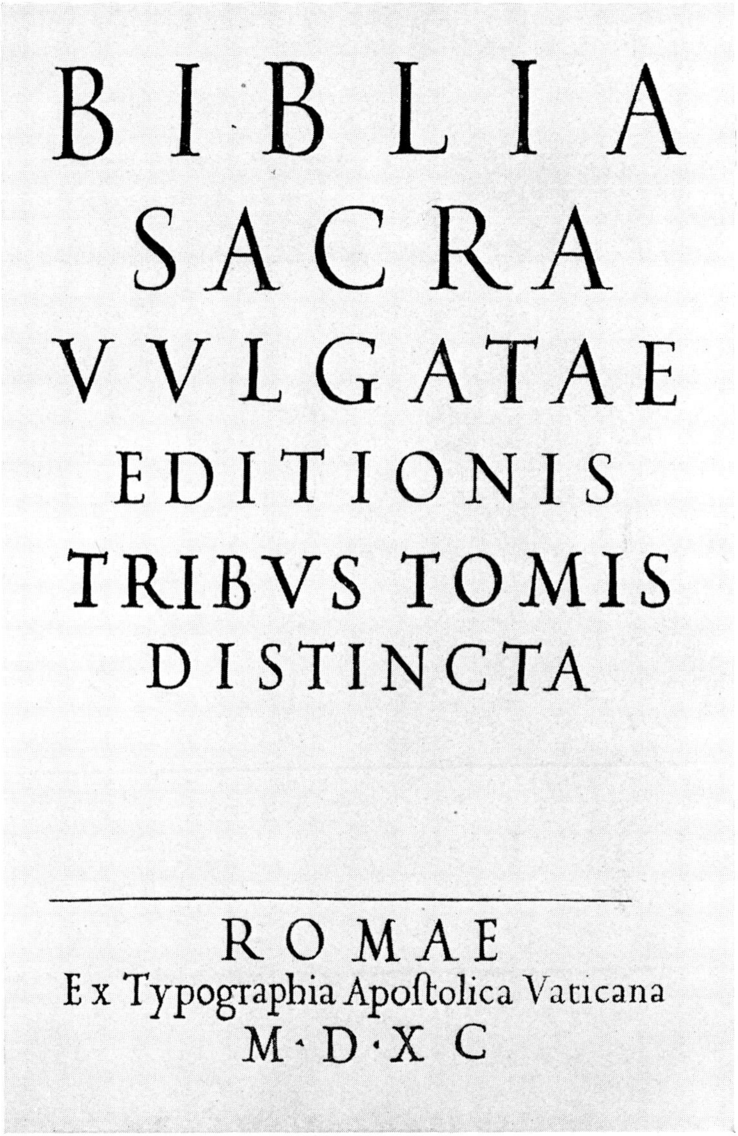

# BIBLIA SACRA VVLGATAE EDITIONIS TRIBVS TOMIS DISTINCTA

ROMAE

Ex Typographia Apoſtolica Vaticana

M·D·X C

*Biblia Sacra*

Rome: Ex Typographia Vaticana, 1590

$12\frac{3}{4}'' \times 8\frac{3}{8}''$

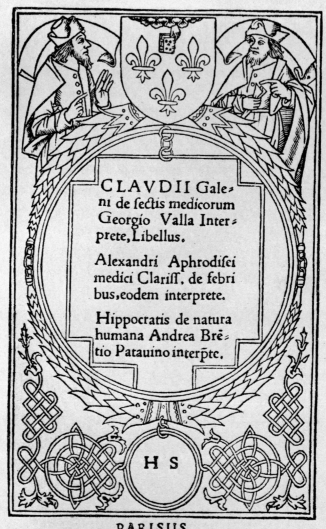

CLAVDII Gale=
ni de fectis medicorum
Georgio Valla Inter=
prete, Libellus.

Alexandri Aphrodifei
medici Clariff. de febri
bus,eodem interprete.

Hippocratis de natura
humana Andrea Brē=
tio Patauino interpte.

H S

PARISIIS
In officina Henrici Stephani.

Galenus: *De Sectis Medicorum*

Paris: H. Estienne, 1518

$6\frac{1}{2}'' \times 3\frac{7}{8}''$

ARS VERSIFICATORIA HVLDERI
CI HVTTENI.

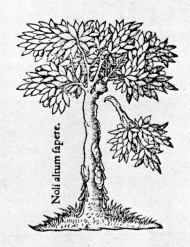

Noli altum sapere.

PARISIIS.
EX OFFICINA ROBERTI STEPHA=
NI EREGIONE SCHOLAE DECRE
TORVM.
M.D.XXVIII.

Ulrich von Hutten: *Ars Versificatoria*

Paris: R. Estienne, 1528

$4\frac{1}{2}'' \times 2\frac{5}{8}''$

# G. Budæi Parisiensis Cõ-

SILIARII REGII, SVPPLICVMQ.
libellorum in Regia magiſtri, Ad inuiⁱⁱⁱⁱⁱⁱⁱ. & poten-
tiſſ. principem Franciſcũ Chriſtianiſſ. regem Franciæ

# DE TRANSITV

## Helleniſmi ad Chriſti-
aniſmum, Libri tres.

P A R I S I I S.
Ex officina Rob. Stephani.
M. D. XXXV.

# Cum priuilegio Regis.

Budé: *De Transitu Hellenismi ad Christianismum*

Paris: R. Estienne, 1535

$8\frac{1}{8}'' \times 4\frac{1}{2}''$

# DE TRANSITV
## Hellenifmi ad Chrifti-
## anifmum, Lib. primus.

ONSIDERANTI MI-
hi fæpenumero, Fracifce rex po-
tetiffime, ad eamque mentis inte
tione vehementer incubeti, quod-
nam dignum operæpreciu ex vfu
philologiæ, atque è literarum co
fuetudine ferre poffem: & verò
fcire auenti quo pacto potiffimu
meliore hominis interioris con-
ditione, ex eo labore ftudióq; efficere, cui externa & corporis bona quæ dicta funt, pofthabeda, ætate quoque flo-
rentiffima duxeram: cupiditas inceffit adeundæ tandem &
confuledæ philofophiæ. Philofophia aute (inquit apud
Platonem Socrates in Phædone) mortis eft meditatio, eò
demum ipfa fpectans, vt anima corpori nunc cofociata,
hinc tandem fublimis abeat, corporifque contagione de-
functa morte facili, ad deum creatore fuum rapiatur, cuius illa fimilitudine ab eodem ipfo prædita eft, quàm fieri poteft integerrima ab ipfius corporis focietate. & quidem ipfius philofophiæ munus eft, id quod homines no-
runt difcendi cupidiffimi, animam vt hominis docedam
fufcipiat, corpori alligatam, atque illi conglutinatam, &
verò neceffariò coactam, quafiper carcerem quendam, fic
A.i.

Budé: *De Transitu Hellenismi ad Christianismum*

Paris: R. Estienne, 1535

$7\frac{3}{8}'' \times 4\frac{1}{2}''$

# Naturæ præpofitionũ ex Prifciano.

Πλίον ἰλαιο ἰ ὄίνο,
Plus olei quàm vini.

P A R I S I I S.
Apud Franciſcum Stephanum.
M.D.X X X V I I I.

Priscianus: *Naturae Praepositionum*

Paris: F. Estienne, 1538

$5\frac{1}{8}'' \times 2\frac{3}{4}''$

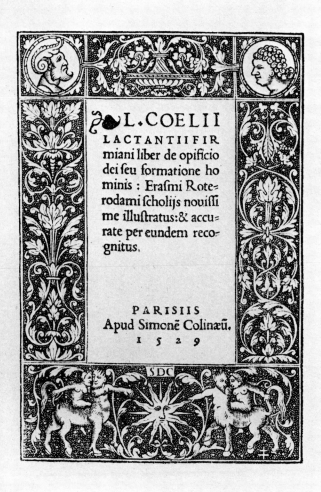

Lactantius: *De Opificio Dei*

Paris: S. de Colines, 1529

$4\frac{7}{8}'' \times 3\frac{3}{8}''$

GENERALE DECRETVM, CONTINENS
hæresum quæ nūc pullulant species:earum detestationem,modum
iudicandi ac discernendi hereticos,ac relapsos,formam & ordinem
procedendi contra eosdem:eorundem etiam acerbas pœnas,ac de=
mum exhortatiōe ad principes potestatesǫ seculares: de illis pro=
fligandis & exterminandis.

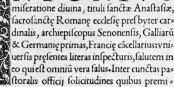

NTONIVS
miseratione diuina, tituli sanctæ Anastasiæ,
sacrosanctę Romanę ecclesię presbyter car=
dinalis, archiepiscopus Senonensis, Galliarū
& Germanię primas,Francię cācellarius:vni=
uersis presentes literas inspecturis,salutem in
eo quiest omniū vera salus.Inter cunctas pa=
storalis officij solicitudines quibus premi=
mur incessanter,illa fortius nos angit:vt cūctis hereticis de finibus Chri
stianorū expulsis,suisǫ falsis & virulentis scriptis ac pestilentibus doctri
nis,penitus extirpatis:fides catholica(quæ solidę semper fuit subnixa pe=
træ)integra illibataǫ permaneat. ac populus Christianus nostræ potissi=
mū prouinciæ: in fidei syncæritate(quolibet obscuritatis semoto velami
ne) immobilis inuiolatusǫ persistat. Sane prospicientes(quod non sine
graui displicentia referimus) insurrexisse nonnullos pseudochristos ac=
pseudoprophetas,quorum dux & vexillifer est Martinus Lutherus: qui
a veritate excidentes,nonnullos ac pene infinitos,etiam si fieri possit,ele=
ctos(vt est apud Matthæum) ad errores inducunt homines.haud dubie  *Matth.24.*
hæresiarchas fastuosos:seditiosos,luciferiana superbia ac rabie lupina ere
ctos.ac demum quales apostolus ad Timothæū graphice describit:suisǫ  *1.Timo.4.*
pingit coloribus,& adamussim exprimit.Qui rursus(vt inquit Petrus)  *2.Petri.2.*
sectas perditas ac damnatas introducunt : libertatem promittentes, cum
ipsi sint serui corruptionis,in maximam certe reipublicę Christianę per=
niciem & iacturam: ac tādem nisi cito occurratur, ruinam & euersiōe.
Vtpote quos non pudet nouas hęreses effingere:sed etiā satagunt ac stu=
dent veteres, & iam diu per ecclesiā sopitas,instaurare.Et inter hæc, pri=
mum de sacramentis ecclesiæ multa perniciose dogmatisant:affirmantes
laicos & mulierculas, æque atǫ presbyteros,posse absoluere. Et quod
hactenus fuit inauditū:laicis vt sacerdotibus,eucharistiæ consecrationem
permittūt.Inter sacerdotes & plebem,nihil interesse dicūt:sed omnes sa=
cerdotes putant, quicunǫ sunt Christiani. In clericis,in sacris ordinibus

*Decreta Prov. Conc. Senonensis*

Paris: S. de Colines, 1529

$9\frac{1}{8}'' \times 5\frac{7}{8}''$

4

## ❧CLAVDII CLAVDIANI POETAE ILLVSTRISS. DE RAPTV PROSERPI- NAE LIBER PRIMVS.

Nferni raptoris equos,afflatáſʒ curru
Sidera tænario, caligantéſʒ profundæ
Iunonis thalamos audaci promere cätu
Mens congeſta iubet.greſſus remoue-
te prophani.

i

Iam furor humanos noſtro de pectore ſenſus
Expulit,& totum ſpirant præcordia Phœbum.
Iam mihi cernuntur trepidis deſubra moueri
Sedibus,& claram diſpergere lumine lucem,
Aduentum teſtata dei. iam magnus ab imis
Auditur fremitus terris,templúmʒ remugit
Cecropidum,ſanctaſʒ faces extollit Eleuſis.
Angues Triptolemi ſtrident,& ſquamea curnis
Colla leuant aſtricta iugis:lapſúʒ ſereno
Erecti,roſeas tendunt ad carmina criſtas.
¸ Ecce procul ternis Hecate variata figuris
Exoritur:letúſʒ ſimul procedit Iacchus
Crinali florens hedera:quem Parthica tigris
Velat,& auratos in nodum colligit vngues.
Ebria Mœonijs figit veſtigia Thyrſis
Dij, quibus in numerum vacui famulantur auerni,
Vulgus iners opibus quorum donatur auaris
Quicquid in orbe petit,quos ſtyx liuentibus ambit
Iterfuſa vadis,& quos fumantia torquens

a.iiij.

Claudianus: *Opuscula*
Paris: S. de Colines, 1530
$5\frac{3}{8}'' \times 2\frac{3}{4}''$

Orontius Fine: *Quadrans Astrolabicus*

Paris: S. de Colines, 1534

$8\frac{7}{8}'' \times 6\frac{1}{2}''$

# VALERIVS
## MAXIMVS.

ADDITO INDICE PERBREVI, CEV
AD OMNEIS HISTORIAS ASY,
LO TVTISSIMO.

PARISIIS
**Apud Simonem Colinæum.**
1 5 3 5

Valerius Maximus: *Opera*
Paris: S. de Colines, 1535
$4\frac{1}{2}'' \times 2\frac{1}{2}''$

Cicero: *Officia*

Paris: S. de Colines, 1543

$4'' \times 2\frac{1}{2}''$

2

## ⸎MARCI TVLLII CICE⸗
### RONIS DE OFFICIIS
*Lib. primus, ad* M. *filium.*

ARGVMENTVM PER ERAS⸗
MVM ROTERODAMVM.

Ciceronem filium ſuo hortatur exēplo ne ſim-
plici cuipiam ſtudio ſeſe addicat, ſed Græca cum
Latinis, & orationis virtutes cū philoſophiæ ſciē
tia coniungat. deinde quò eum reddat attentio-
rem, hanc, quæ de officiis eſt philoſophiæ partem,
duobus potiſſimum nominibus cōmendat, vel quòd
vſus eius ad omnem vitæ rationem latiſſime pa⸗
teat, vel quòd hæc vna ſit philoſophis omnibus
inter ſe cōmunis. Poſtremo teſtatur ſe in hac diſ-
putatione Stoicos potiſſimū ſequi, quòd hi vel opti
me boni finem, ad quem officia omnia referun-
tur, conſtituerint : quum Epicurus voluptate me-
tiens ſummum bonum, atq; Ariſto, Pyrrho & He-
rillus tollentes rerum delectum, officiū quoque na-
turam ſubuerterint.

¶ Vanquam te Marce fili annum iam au-
dientem Cratippū (idque Athenis) abū-
dare oportet præceptis inſtitutiſque philoſophiæ, propter ſummam & doctoris authori-
tatem, & vrbis:quorum alter te ſcientia augere
poteſt, altera exemplis : tamen vt ipſe ad meam

*a.ij.*

Cicero: *Officia*

Paris: S. de Colines, 1543

$3\frac{3}{4}'' \times 2''$

❡ *Figura dioptræ, seu regulæ super instrumenti facie reponendæ.*

*Pinnacidium.*      *Latitudo septentrionalis.*    *Latitudo australis.*

❧TRIVM INSIGNIORVM, ET HACTENVS☙
desideratorum operum Mathematicorum , De Circuli videlicet quadratura, eiúsque dimensione, & ratione circunferentiæ ad dia-
metrum: De regularium insuper & multangularū omnium
figurarum descriptione: Ac de locorum inuenienda longitudinis differétia, aliter quàm per lunares ecli-
pses: Vnà cum Planisphærio geographico:
Authore Orontio Finæo Delphi-
nate, Regio Mathema-
ticarum Lutetiæ
professore,

F I N I S.

☙IOANNIS ROVETII SENONENSIS,
Medici, in Orontiomastigem,
scazon.

Z oile Gigantum frater, ecquid omnibus
Omnia miser sic inuides? dic perdites?
Cur inuides illi inuidiam, qui non tibi
Illam inuidet? Qui sis studebo prodere
Vt miseriorem, quàm putes, omnibus ego
Te faciam. Habet F I N AE V S insignem Genium,
Non patitur vt te nominem: ne forte tibi
Fortuna plaudens iure succenseat. Age,
Si nomen edo, ne malè hoc tibi inuideas,
Timendum etiam fuerit: ero quod tibi minùs
Esse potes. aude pauca, non paucos habet
F I N AE V S amicos. Tu deum hostem ac homines.

❡ *Errata aliquot notatu digniora, impressoriæ artis*
*labilitate commissa.*
Facie 39, Corollario 3: legendum (vt 3 & $\frac{2}{15}$, ad 1)
Facie 48, linea 2: legendum, triangulo a b c, circunscripto.

❡Registrum huius operis
3 3 3 4 4 4 3 3 3.
☙ A B C D E F G H.

Orontius Fine: *Quadratura Circuli*

Paris: S. de Colines, 1544

9″ × 5″

à mutis,quod aiūt,magiſtris acceptas,octo & viginti annos Lutetiæ publicè docen-
do,interpretando,ſcriptis & nouis inuētionibus exornādo illuſtraui)pretium operæ
faĉturum me putaui,ſi nodū hunc diſſoluerē,& Galliam tuam ſub tuo fælici nomine,hoc rariſſimo munere donarem.Q uod (ni me fallit ipſa veritas,& Mathematicarum inexpugnabilis certitudo)à diuina tandē impetraui clemētia.Ipſam nanq̃
Circuli quadraturā,via haĉtenus à nemine tentata,& methodo inaudita,clariſſi-
mè demonſtraui,atq̃ non vni tantūmodò Circulo æquale quadratū,ſed tribus Cir=
culis tria ſimul æqualia quadrata,vel è diuerſo,figurare docui:totūmq̃ inuentionis
ac demōſtrationis artificiū,quinq̃ problematibus,& vnica, eáq̃ ſimpliciſſima,con-
cluſi figuræ contextura.Ex ipſo autem primo problemate,à Græcis olim tot modis
inueſtigata,ſed nōdū planè demōſtrata Cubi duplicatio,euidētiſſimè colligetur.Huic
porrò Circuli tetragoniſmo,duas adiunxi demonſtrationes:alteram de ipſius Circuli
dimenſione,alteram verò de ratione cincunferentiæ ad diametrum:quæ tot fælicia
ingenia,vt Circulo æquale darent quadratum,haĉtenus defatigarunt. Subſequitur
deinde abſolutum,& à nemine anteà tentatum opus,de multāgularum omnium &
regularium figurarum deſcriptione: quo bona pars ipſius Geometriæ,quæ priùs la=
tebat,& ſupramodum vtilis videbatur,in poſterum fiet manifeſta.Acceſſit tandem
liber admodùm eximius, de inuenienda longitudinis locorū differentia,aliter quàm
per Lunares eclipſes,etiam dato quouis tempore:vnà cū Planiſphærio geographico,
recēns itidem excogitato.Q uem librū anno ſuperiore,gallicè conſcriptum,vnà cum
Delphinatus,Prouinciæ,Sabaudiæ,& Pedemontanæ regionis Corographia,tuæ ob-
tuli maieſtati.Hæc igitur inſignia totiéſq̃ deſiderata Mathematū opera tria,ſub
tuo fælici nomine & auſpicio,in publicum tandē prodire ſum paſſus:Q uæ tibi Ma
thematicarum,ac reliquarum bonarū artium raro Mecœnati,térq̃ maximo Principi
(nempe Regū Chriſtianiſſimo,potētiſſimo,ac omni virtutū genere animíq̃ dexteri-
tate prædito)candidè deuoueo,& protegenda cōmitto. An verò palmā hanc præter
multorū ſpem,reportaturus ſim:cuius æquo lectori,& in Mathematicis non infæ-
liciter verſato,cenſendum relinquo. Cuperem tamen de multis, hîc te vnicum habere iudicem:ſi per humanitatem tuam,& publicas occupationes,quibus hoc impor=
tuno tempore (in quo Mars ſuis comitatus Furijs,longè latéq̃ fremit)valde diſtrin
geris,me ipſum interpretem audire graue nō eſſet:qui & de rebus omnibus recĕ iu-
dicare, & illas æqui boníque conſulere abunde noſti. Reliquum eſt, clementiſſime
Rex,vt tui Orontij ſic tandem meminiſſe pergas:vt cum in inſtaurandis,& (te
auſpice)docēdis Mathematicis,annos meliores conſumpſiſſe non pœniteat. Vale.

Lutetiæ Pariſiorum, Menſe Iulio, 1 5 4 4.

Orontius Fine: *Quadratura Circuli*

Paris: S. de Colines, 1544

$8\frac{3}{8}'' \times 5\frac{1}{8}''$

# Chriſtianiſſimo Galloꝛ̃ Regi,

## FRANCISCO, EIVS NOMI-
### nis primo, Orontius Finæus Delphinas, S. D.

IVINA PROVIDENTIA
*factum eſſe puto, FRANCISCE Rex
Chriſtianiſſime, vt quæ præclara ſunt & dif
ficilia, quantò magis ab ipſis deſiderantur &
perquiruntur hominibus: tantò tardiùs à pau
cis plurimùm inueniantur, & in ſua diffe-
rantur tempora, illiſque deſtinentur inuento-
ribus, quos ſolus Deus ad hæc nouit eſſe dele-
ctos. Cum ob multa, tum vt igneus & planè*
cæleſtis ille diuini ſplendoris vigor, mentibus
noſtris inſitus, magis atque magis elucescat : & ad perſcrutanda latentium rerum
arcana acriori nos vrgeat ſtimulo, in illorúmque aſſidua contemplatione & indagatione fixam oblectet intelligẽtiam. Quod ſi tam in diuinis & naturalibus, quàm
mechanicis & ciuilibus rebus, locum habere compertum eſt: in ijs artibus, quæ ſolæ
Mathematicæ, hoc eſt, diſciplinæ nũcupari merueru̅t, vſu maximè venire (opinor)
negabit nemo . Quanquam enim ipſæ Mathematicæ, medium inter intellectilia
ſenſiliáque locum obtinentes, cæteris artibus tum fide & ordine, tum certitudine ac
integritate ( præter ſummam quæ illis ineſt vtilitatem ) longè præſtare viden-
tur: rariores nihilominus ſemper habuere profeſſores, & inſigniora theoremata, ma-
iori cum difficultate , longioríque temporis ſucceſſu adinuenta atque demonſtrata.
Quemadmodum in ea diſciplina, quæ Geometria vocitatur, de Circuli licet intueri
quadratura. Quæ tametſi ab omnibus philoſophis ſciẽtia cõtineri fuerit exiſtimata,
& tãto tempore à tam doctis perquiſita viris: hactenus tamen videtur fuiſſe deſiderata , facta interim non modica rerum Mathematicarum acceſſione: multa enim
ſcitu digniſſima, quæ prius erant abſconſa, prodiere nota. Cùm igitur præfatam
Circuli quadraturam, extra artem non eſſe intelligerem, & illius inuentionẽ ad me
non ſine diuino numine iure quodam deuolui: qui & patre philoſopho ac Mathema-
tico inſigni Franciſco Finæo ſum natus, & ad has diſciplinas natura factus ( quas

B.ij.

Orontius Fine: *Quadratura Circuli*

Paris: S. de Colines, 1544

$8\frac{5}{8}'' \times 5\frac{1}{8}''$

# Q. Horatij flacci

## ODARVM SIVE CARMINVM LIBRI QVATVOR.

*Epodon Liber vnus.*

*Cum annotatiunculis q̃ antea auctioribus in margine adiectis, quæ breuis comentarij vice esse possint.*

*Nicolai Perotti libellus non infrugifer de metris Odarum Horatianarum.*

TEM PVS.

VIRTVS.SOLA·ACIEM
RETVNDIT.ISTAM

PARISIIS.
Apud Simonem Colinæum.
1 5 3 9

Horatius

Paris: S. de Colines, 1539

$5\frac{1}{4}'' \times 2\frac{3}{4}''$

## Q. HORATII FLACCI VITA PER PETRVM CRINITVM FLORENTINVM.

Q Horatius Flaccus in Venusio Apuliæ oppi-
do natus est : patrem habuit Libertini generis. Vnde illud,

Quem rodunt omnes Libertino patre natum.
Pro certo habetur eius natalem fuisse duobus circiter
annis ante coniurationem L. Sergij Catilinæ, quo tempore celebres erant in ciuitate, ex Poëtis Val. Catullus, Licinius Caluus, & Heluius Cinna: ex oratoribus
M. Cicero, Q. Hortensius, & Q. Catulus: ex phi-
losophis Var. Terentius, & Figulus Nigidius. Orbilium
Beneuentanum, vt constat, à puero audiuit, quem ap-
pellat alicubi plagosum, ac mirum quàm breui tempore
in bonis literis profecerit. Ingenio enim facili, & aui-
dissimo fuisse traditur in capiendis optimis disciplinis.
Vbi autê satis visus est nauasse operâ Latinis studijs,
Athenas se côtulit, vt Philosophorũ præceptis liberius
incumberet, maximéẽ Epicureorum placita videtur
probasse, vt illud vrbanè dictum testatur:

Me pinguem, & nitidum bene curata cute vises,
Cum ridere voles Epicuri de grege porcum.
Moribus fuisse dicitur subobscœnis, & ad bilem inter-
dum paulo excitatior: adeo erga amicos gratus, atque
officiosus, vt nobiliorum etiam studijs & gratia clarior
in dies, ac nobilior esset. Nam primò dignitatem Tri-
buniitiam honestis suffragijs est adeptus, & Romanæ

a.ij.

Horatius

Paris: S. de Colines, 1539

$5\frac{1}{2}'' \times 2\frac{3}{4}''$

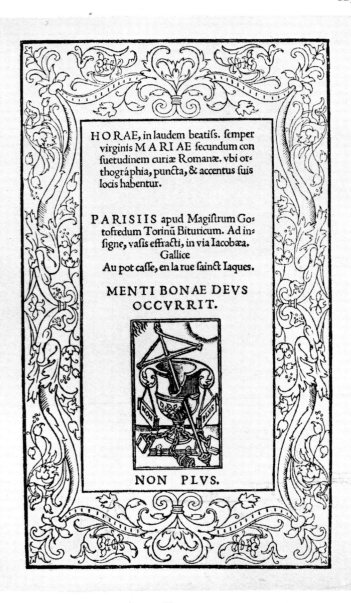

HORAE, in laudem beatiſſ. ſemper
virginis MARIAE ſecundum con
ſuetudinem curiæ Romanæ. vbi or=
thográphia, punĉta, & accentus ſuis
locis habentur.

PARISIIS apud Magiſtrum Go=
tofredum Torinũ Bituricum. Ad in=
ſigne, vaſis effraĉti, in via Iacobæa.
Gallice
Au pot caſſe, en la rue ſainĉt Iaques.

MENTI BONAE DEVS
OCCVRRIT.

NON PLVS.

*Horae*

Paris: Geofroy Tory, 1525

$6\frac{3}{8}'' \times 3\frac{7}{8}''$

I

*Horae*

Paris: Geofroy Tory, 1525

$6\frac{1}{2}'' \times 3\frac{3}{4}''$

*Horae*

Paris: Geofroy Tory, 1529

$3\frac{3}{8}'' \times 2''$

*Horae*

Paris: Geofroy Tory, 1529

$3\frac{1}{2}'' \times 1\frac{7}{8}''$

*Horae*

Paris: Geofroy Tory, 1529

$3\frac{1}{4}'' \times 1\frac{7}{8}''$

*Horae*

Paris: M. Fezandat, 1547

$3\frac{1}{2}'' \times 1\frac{3}{4}''$

¶ Euangile selon Sainct Iean, qu'on
dict le iour de Noel.

AV commence-
ment estoit la
parolle, & la parolle
estoit auec Dieu, &
Dieu estoit la parol
le. Icelle estoit auec
Dieu dés le cōmēce
mēt. Toutes choses
sōt faictes par icelle
& sans icelle riē n'a
esté fait de ce qui est
faict. En icelle estoit
la vie: & la vie estoit
la lumiere des hōes,
& la lumiere luyt aux
tenebres: mais les te
nebres ne l'ont point cōprinse. Vn homme fut en-
uoyé de Dieu, qui estoit nommé Iean. Cestuy est
venu en tesmoignage, pour rendre tesmoignage
de la lumiere: à fin que to⁹ creussent par icelle. Cestuy n'estoit point la lumiere, mais estoit pour rendre tesmoignage de la lumiere. La vraye lumiere
estoit celle qui enlumine tout homme venant en
ce monde. Elle estoit au monde, & le monde est
faict par icelle, mais le monde ne l'a pas cogneue.
Elle estoit venue és choses qui estoient siennes, &
les siennes ne l'ont point receue. Mais tous ceux
qui l'ont receue, elle leur a donné puissance d'estre

*Horae*

Paris: Magdeleine Boursette, 1554

$4\frac{3}{4}'' \times 2\frac{7}{8}''$

*Horae*

Paris: Magdeleine Boursette, 1554

$4\frac{3}{4}'' \times 3''$

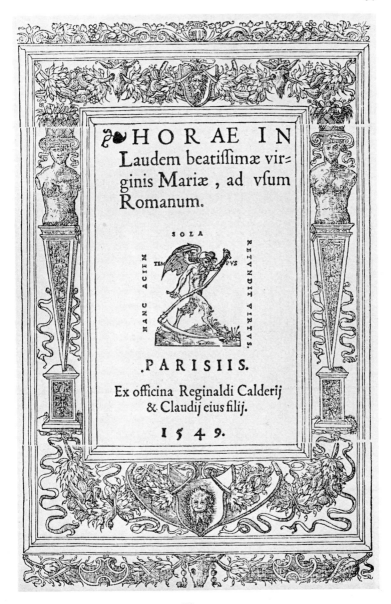

*Horae*

Paris: Chauldière, 1549

$8\frac{1}{4}'' \times 5\frac{1}{4}''$

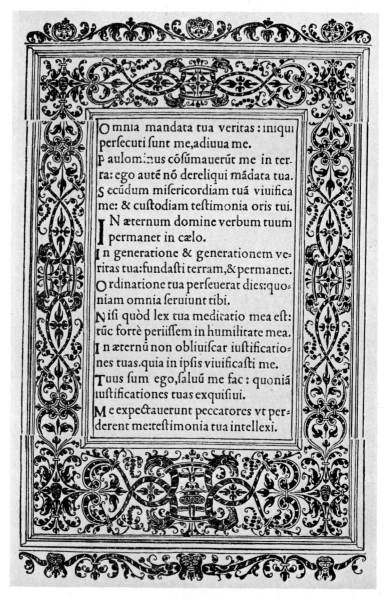

Omnia mandata tua veritas : iniqui perfecuti funt me,adiuua me.

paulominus côfumauerût me in terra: ego auté nô dereliqui mâdata tua.

Secûdum mifericordiam tuâ viuifica me: & cuftodiam teftimonia oris tui.

IN æternum domine verbum tuum permanet in cælo.

In generatione & generationem veritas tua:fundafti terram,& permanet.

Ordinatione tua perfeuerat dies:quoniam omnia feruiunt tibi.

Nifi quòd lex tua meditatio mea eft: tûc fortè periiffem in humilitate mea.

In æternû non obliuifcar iuftificationes tuas.quia in ipfis viuificafti me.

Tuus fum ego,faluû me fac : quoniâ iuftificationes tuas exquifiui.

Me expectauerunt peccatores vt perderent me:teftimonia tua intellexi.

*Horae*

Paris: Chauldière, 1549

$7\frac{7}{8}'' \times 5''$

*Horae*

Paris: Guillaume Merlin, 1552

$4\frac{3}{4}'' \times 2\frac{7}{8}''$

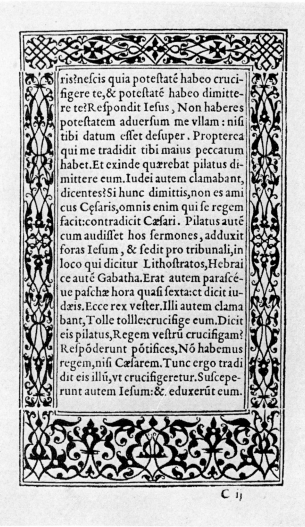

ris?nefcis quia poteftaté habeo cruci-
figere te, & poteftaté habeo dimitte-
re te?Refpondit Iefus, Non haberes
poteftatem aduerfum me vllam : nifi
tibi datum effet defuper. Propterea
qui me tradidit tibi maius peccatum
habet.Et exinde quærebat pilatus di-
mittere eum.Iudei autem clamabant,
dicentes?Si hunc dimittis,non es ami
cus Cefaris,omnis enim qui fe regem
facit:contradicit Cæfari. Pilatus auté
cum audiffet hos fermones, adduxit
foras Iefum, & fedit pro tribunali,in
loco qui dicitur Lithoftratos,Hebrai
ce auté Gabatha.Erat autem parafcé-
ue pafchæ hora quafi fexta:et dicit iu-
dæis.Ecce rex vefter.Illi autem clama
bant,Tolle tollle:crucifige eum.Dicit
eis pilatus,Regem veftrŭ crucifigam?
Refpóderunt pótifices,Nó habemus
regem,nifi Cæfarem.Tunc ergo tradi
dit eis illŭ,vt crucifigeretur.Sufcepe-
runt autem Iefum:&. eduxerŭt eum.

C ij

*Horae*

Paris: Guillaume Merlin, 1552

$4\frac{3}{4}'' \times 2\frac{7}{8}''$

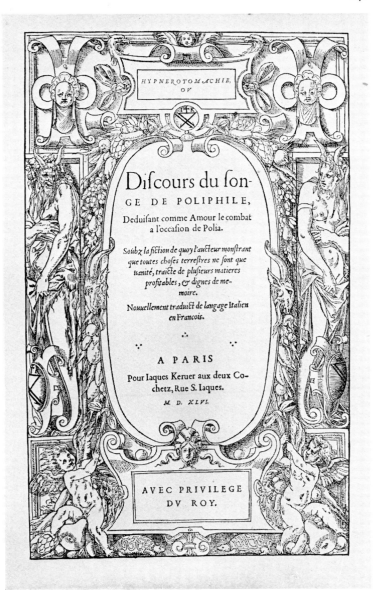

*Songe de Poliphile*

Paris: Jacques Kerver, 1546

$11\frac{1}{4}'' \times 7\frac{1}{4}''$

# Poliphile craignant le peril de la

## FOREST, FEIT SON ORAISON A IVPITER:

*puis en trouua l'yſſue, tout alteré de ſoif. Et ainſi qu'il ſe uouloit rafraichir en une fon-*
*taine, il ouyt un chant melodieux, pour lequel ſuiure abandonna l'eau preſte:*
*dont il ſe trouua puisapres en plus grande angoiſſe que deuant.*

Bſuſqué de mon entendement, ſans pouuoir co-
gnoiſtre quel party ie deuoie prendre, ou mourir en ceſte foreſt eſgarée, ou eſperer mon ſalut
incertain, ie faiſoie tout mon effort d'en yſſir:
mais tant plus alloie auãt, plus entroy ie en grã-
des tenebres, fort foible, & trêblant pour la peur
que i'auoie : car ie n'attêdoie ſinon que quelque
beſte me vint afronter pour me deuorer: ou que
heurtaſt du pied à vn tronc ou racine, ie tumbaſſe
dans quelque abyſme, & feuſſe englouti de la terre, côme fut Amphiaraus.
En ceſte maniere ſe troubloit mon entêdement, ſans eſperance, & ſans rai-
ſon, errant ſans voie ny ſentier. Parquoy voiant qu'en mon faict n'y auoit
autre remede, ie me voys recommander a la diuine miſericorde, diſant, O
Dieſpiter treſgrãd, treſbô, treſpuiſſant, & treſſecourable, ſi p hûbles & deuo-
tes prieres l'humanite peult meriter le ſecours des diuins ſuffrages, & doit
eſtre de vous exaucee, ie apreſent repentãt & dolêt de toutes mes fragilitez
& offenſes paſſees, vous ſupplie & inuoque, ſouuerain pere eternel, recteur
du ciel & de la terre, qu'il plaiſe a voſtre deité incôprehêſible, me deſiurer de
ces perilz, ſi que ie puiſſe acheuer le cours de ma vie par quelque autre me-
lieure fin.   A peine eu ie finé mon oraiſon bien deuotemêt proferée, & d'vn
cueur tout humilié, les yeulx pleins de larmes, croiant fermemêt q̃ les dieux
ſecourent & ſauuent ceulx qui les inuoquent de pure volûté, que ie me trouuay hors de la foreſt: dont tout ainſi que ſi d'vne nuict froide & humide ie
feuſſe paruenu en vn iour clair & ſerain, mes yeulx ſortans de telle obſcuri-
té, ne pouuoient bien (pour quelque temps) ſouffrir la clairté du ſoleil. I'e-
ſtoie haſſé, triſte, & angoiſſeux, tant qu'il ſembloit proprement que ie ſor-
tiſſe d'une baſſe ſoſſe, preſque tout rôpu & briſé de chaines & de fers, chan-
gé de viſage, debile, & de cueur alenty, en ſorte que n'eſtimoie plus rien tout
cela qui m'eſtoit preſent. Oultre ce i'auoie telle ſoif, que l'air fraiz & delicat
ne me pouuoit aucunemêt rafraichir, ny ſatiſfaire a la ſechereſſe de ma bouche. Mais apres auoir reprins vn petit de courage, par toutes manieres deli-
beray d'appaiſer ceſte ſoif: parquoy allay querant parmy celle contrée, tant
que ie trouuay vne groſſe veine d'eau fraiche, ſourdant & bouillonnant en
vne belle fontaine, qui couloit par vn petit ruyſſeau, lequel deuenoit vne
riuiere bruyante atrauers les pierres & troncz des arbres tumbez & ren-
uerſez en ſon canal, & contre leſquelz celle eau ſe regorgeoit comme cour-
roucée & marrie de ce qu'ilz la cuidoient retarder, elle qui eſtoit augmen-
tée de pluſieurs autres ruyſſeletz, auec aucuns torrens engendrez des neiges
fondues, precipitees des montaignes, qui ne ſembloient eſtre gueres loing,

*Songe de Poliphile*

Paris: Jacques Kerver, 1546

$10\frac{3}{4}'' \times 5\frac{3}{4}''$

DE AMADIS DE GAVLE.    Fueillet.I.

# Le premier liure de Amadis de Gaule,

Traduict d'Espaignol en Françoys, par le Seigneur des Essars.

Quelz furent les Roys Garinter & Perion , & d'vn combat
qu'eut icelluy Perion par cas fortuit contre deux cheualiers:
puis contre vn Lyon qui deuoroit vn Cerf en leur presence,
& de ce qu'il en aduint.

Chapitre premier.

 Eu de temps apres la Passion de nostre Saul-
ueur Iesus Christ, il fut vn Roy de la petite
Bretaigne nommé Garinter, instruict en la loy
de verité, & grandement decoré de bonnes &
louables vertuz, qui eut d'vne noble dame son
espouse, deux filles. Laisnée (mariée auec Languines Roy d'Escoce) communement appellée la dame de la Guirlande: par ce que le Roy
son mary , pour la beaulté de ses cheueulx , &
le grand plaisir qu'il prenoit à les veoir, ne les
luy permettoit couurir, sinon auec vn petit cercle ou chapelet de fleurs. De
ce Roy Languines & d'elle , furent engendrez Agraies & Mabile , des-
quelz l'hystoire presente fera souuent mention. L'aultre fille puisnée de ce
Roy Garinter, nommée Elisene fut trop plus belle que son aisnée. Et combien qu'elle eust esté maintesfois demandée & requise en mariaige de plusieurs princes & grans seigneurs: neantmoins ne luy en print ( pour lors)
aulcun vouloir,  ains par sa solitude , & saincte vie , estoit communement
A        appellée

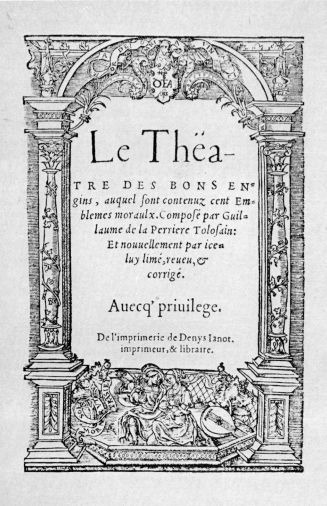

G. de la Perrière: *Le Théâtre des Bons Engins*

Paris: Denys Janot, 1539

$4\frac{7}{8}'' \times 3\frac{1}{4}''$

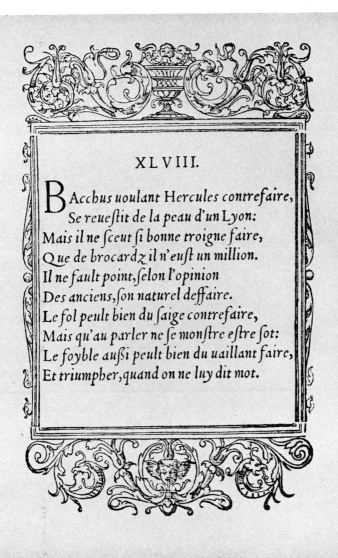

## XLVIII.

Bacchus uoulant Hercules contrefaire,
Se reueſtit de la peau d'un Lyon:
Mais il ne ſceut ſi bonne troigne faire,
Que de brocardʒ il n'euſt un million.
Il ne fault point, ſelon l'opinion
Des anciens, ſon naturel deffaire.
Le fol peult bien du ſaige contrefaire,
Mais qu'au parler ne ſe monſtre eſtre ſot:
Le foyble auſſi peult bien du uaillant faire,
Et triumpher, quand on ne luy dit mot.

G. de la Perrière: *Le Théâ.re des Bons Engins*

Paris: Denys Janot, 1539

$5\frac{1}{4}'' \times 3\frac{3}{8}''$

K

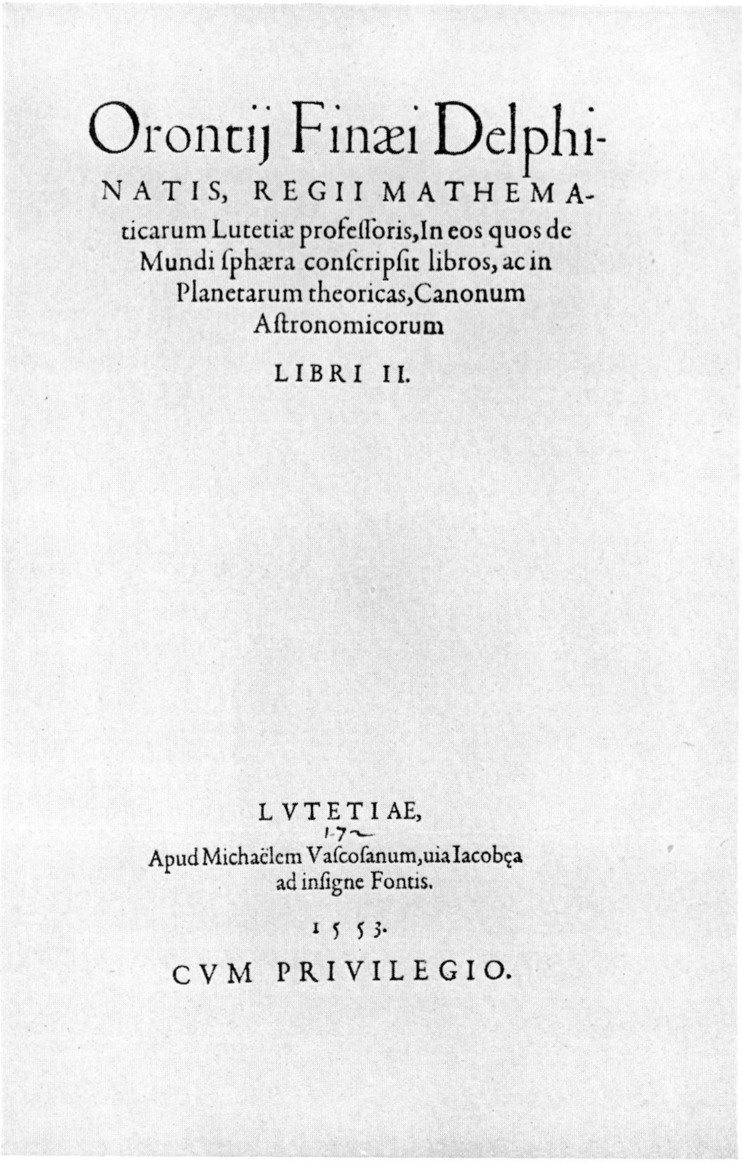

Orontij Finæi Delphi-
NATIS, REGII MATHEMA-
ticarum Lutetiæ profeſſoris, In eos quos de
Mundi ſphæra conſcripſit libros, ac in
Planetarum theoricas, Canonum
Aſtronomicorum

LIBRI II.

LVTETIAE,
Apud Michaëlem Vaſcoſanum, uia Iacobęa
ad inſigne Fontis.

1553.

CVM PRIVILEGIO.

Orontius Fine: *De Mundi Sphaera*

Paris: M. Vascosan, 1553

$6\frac{3}{8}'' \times 3\frac{7}{8}''$

## CANON XVI. 61

partes ipſius primi numeri, uertuntur in partes 7, & minuta

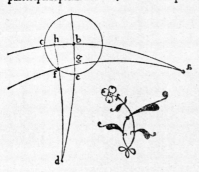

11,25,ferè. Tã
tus eſt igitur
ſinus rectus
quæſitę ęqua
tionis ƒ g: cu
ius arcus of-
fendetur ha-
bere grad° 6,
& min. 52,58.
Atqui totidẽ
partium, atq;
minutorũ ex
peritur eſſe,
quæ in tabu-
lis paſsim di-
uulgatis continetur æquatio, præfato 50 graduum reſpondẽs
argumento. Et quoniam manifeſtum eſt, arcum b h, maiorẽ
eſſe arcu ƒ g: non eſt igitur idem arcus b h, quæſita æquatio
ipſius octauæ ſphæræ, ſed præfatus arcus ƒ g. Haud aliter pe-
riculum facere licebit, de cæterorum quorũcunque argumẽ
torum æquationibus. Hinc poterit ipſa æquationum octauę
ſphæræ tabula, quæ in minutis ſecundis ſæpius peccare uidetur, recenti atque fido magis numerari calculo.

### CANON XVI.

Quantum diſtet uerum initium ſignorum o-
ctauæ ſphæræ, ab ipſo tabulari ſignorũ exor-
dio, tandem ſupputare.

1   Hic ſupponimus Alphonſinam, & omnium ſequẽtium
poſitionem de motu octauæ ſphæræ, ueram ac ſtabilem eſſe,
donec meliorem obtinuerimus excogitationem. Neque in
præſentiarum intendimus ipſam edocere theoricam, utpo-
te, quæ paſsim diuulgata, & luculenter à quamplurimis tra-
dita eſt: Sed ex ipſa ſanè quàm intellecta motus octaui orbis
theorica, calculum Alphonſinum reuocare ad uernalẽ Ecli-

## CAROLO LOTHARINGIO

### S. R. E. CARDINALI ILLVSTRISS.

*Petrus Paschalius S. P. D.*

*VONIAM tu penè vnus scri-
bendæ Henrici Regis historiæ non
solum autor, sed adiutor etiã fuisti;
& virorum quoque quorundam il-
lustrium elogiorum conficiendorum
suasor, Princeps illustrißime: idcir-
co quicquid iam à me est profectum,
proficiscetúrque in posterum, non
magis meum esse duco, quàm tuum. Neque enim illi historiarum libri, quos confecimus, quósque nonnulli doctißimi
viri tantopere probarunt, sunt toti nostri; tui sunt maiore
ex parte, & ex doctißimis tuis commentariis decerpti
Hoc autem regium elogium, quod nondum perfectum, semel atque iterum Henrico Regi perlegisti; sic, vel ipso nutu
(aderam enim ipse præsens) emendasti; vt illud non indi-
gnum quo in manus hominum perueniat, iam tandem iu-
dicem. Quare illo nobis erepto Rege, confectóque hoc eius
elogio, visum mihi, & tibi libitum est, vt id in apertum
nunc demum proferremus; & tãti Regis tam illustres lau-
des ab obliuione hominum, quantùm in nobis esset, atque à
silentio vindicaremus. Quod facio, illúdque interea, dum
nostri temporis integram historiam, maximarum sanè vi-
giliarum opus, contexo, in tuo clarißimo nomine apparere
cupio. Huic ego elogio eius sanctißimi Regis demortui for-*

A ij

Paschalius: *Elogia*

Paris: M. Vascosan, 1560

$8\frac{1}{4}'' \times 4\frac{7}{8}''$

# HENRICI II. GALLIARVM

## *REGIS ELOGIVM, PETRO*

### *PASCHALIO AVTORE.*

ENRICVS II. Galliarum Rex, magni illius Francisci Regis filius, ad duodetriginta annos natus, die suo natali regnū est adeptus. Qui cùm maximi populi, optimi, & fideliſſimi, multorúmque virorum nobiliū ac Principum Principem se eſſe, eóque loco locatum, vt longè futuros omnium casus prospicere sibi oporteret, vidit: certis Principibus viris adhibitis, & nonnullis aliis rerum suarum peritis hominibus, omnibus regni rationibus diligenter prouidit: tantámque imperij sui bene administrandi spem omnibus attulit, vt talem Regem non natura solùm & lege Gallica datum, sed vnum ex multis quasi conquisitum & electum omnes facilè iudicarint. Primùm omnium, vir natura sanctus & religiosus, ne quis suo in regno diuinum Numé, ne quídve

A iiij

Paschalius: *Elogia*

Paris: M. Vascosan, 1560

$8\frac{1}{2}'' \times 5''$

## POMPONII ME-
### LÆ DE SITV ORBIS
#### LIBER II.

Scythia Europæa.     Cap.     I.

Siæ in noſtrũ mare Ta-
nainq́ue vergentis qué
dixi, finis ac ſit⁹ eſt. At
per eúdem amnem in
Mœotida remeãtibus,
ad dextram Europa eſt
modò ſiniſtro latere in
nauigãtium appoſita,
ac Riphæis montibus
(nam & huc illi pertinẽt)proxima. Cadentes aſſi-
duè niues adeò inuia efficiunt , vt vltrà ne viſum
quidem intendentium admittant. Deinde eſt regio ditis admodum ſoli,inhabitabilis tamen quia
Gryphi ſæuum & pertinax ferarum genus,aurum
terra penitus egeſtũ mirè amant , miréque cuſto-
diunt, & ſunt infeſti attingentibus. Hominũ primi ſunt Scythę,Scytharúmque,queis ſinguli ocu-
li eſſe dicuntur,Arimaſpi.Ab eis Eſſedones vſque
ad Mœotida.Huius flexũ Buges amnis ſecat. Aga
thyrſi & Sauromatæ ambiunt: quia pro ſedibus
                                                    plauſtra

Pomponius Mela: *De Situ Orbis*

Paris: Jacques Kerver, 1557

$6\frac{7}{8}'' \times 3\frac{3}{4}''$

ESTREINES

# AV ROY HENRY

III. ENVOYEES A SA MAIESTE
AV MOIS DE DECEMBRE.

A V o v s race de Roys Prince de tant
   de Princes,
   Qui tenez deſſous vous deux ſi grã-
   des prouinces,
   Qui par toute l'Europe eſclairez
   tout ainſi
   Qu'vn beau ſoleil d'eſté de flam-
mes eſclarcy,
   Que l'eſtranger admire & le ſuieɕt honore,
   Et dont la maieſté noſtre ſiecle redore.
A vous qui auez tout, ie ne ſçaurois donner
   Preſent, tant ſoit-il grand, qui vous puiſſe eſtrener,
   La terre eſt preſque voſtre, & dans le ciel vous mettre
   Ie ne ſuis pas vn Dieu, ie ne puis le promettre,
   C'eſt à faire au flateur : ie vous puis mon meſtier
   Promettre ſeulement, de l'encre & du papier.
Ie ne ſuis Courtizan ny vendeur de fumées
   Ie n'ay d'ambition les veines allumées,

D

*Henrici Gallorum Regis Epitaphia*
Paris: Féderic Morel, 1559
$6\frac{3}{4}'' \times 4\frac{1}{2}''$

Marguerite de Navarre: *Heptamerone*

Paris: Benoît Prévost, 1559

$6\frac{7}{8}'' \times 4\frac{5}{8}''$

## LA HVICTIESME IOVRNEE DES

### NOVVELLES DE LA ROYNE DE NAVARRE.

E MATIN VENV, s'enquirent si leur pont s'auancoit fort, & trouuerent que dedans deux ou trois iours il pourroit estre paracheué: ce qui despleut à quelques vns de la cõpagnie: car ils eussent bien desiré, que l'ouurage eust duré plus lon guemet, pour faire durer le contentement qu'ils auoient de leur heureuse vie. Mais voyans qu'ils n'auoient plus que deux ou trois iours de bon temps, se delibererent de ne le perdre pas. Et prierent ma dame Oisille de leur donner la pasture spirituelle, comme elle auoit accoustumé: ce qu'elle feit, mais elle les tint plus long temps, qu'auparauant. Car elle vouloit, auant que partir, auoir mise fin à la Cronicque de sainct Iean. A quoy elle s'aequita si tresbien, qu'il sembloit que le sainct esprit plein d'amour & de douceur, parlast par sa bouche. Et tous enflammez de ce feu, s'en allerent ouyr la grand messe. Et apres disner, ensemble parlans encores de la iournée passée, se deffioiet d'en pouuoir faire vne aussi belle. Et pour y donner ordre, se retirerent chacun en son logis iusques à l'heure, qu'ils allerent à leur chambre des comptes sur le bureau de l'herbe verde, ou des-ia trouuerent les moynes

Ff iij

Marguerite de Navarre: *Heptamerone*

Paris: Benoît Prévost, 1559

$6\frac{7}{8}'' \times 4''$

LIVRE
De Perspectiue de Iehan Cousin
Senonois, maistre Painctre à Paris.

STANTE. ETCVRRENTE ROTA.

A PARIS.

De l'Imprimerie de Iehan le Royer Imprimeur du Roy
és Mathématiques.
1560.

AVEC PRIVILEGE DV ROY.

Cousin: *Livre de Perspective*

Paris: Jehan le Royer,  1560

$10\frac{1}{2}'' \times 6\frac{1}{4}''$

## IEHAN COVSIN AV LECTEVR.

AMY Lecteur tu as icy vn mien œuure, contenant les premieres Reigles de l'art de Perspectiue, que i'eusse volunties defiré & adreßé au Roy ou à quelques Princes & grans Seigneurs, selon que couslumierement il se faict, si i'euße senty de l'eloquéce & sçauoir aßez en moy pour m'y oser adreßer. Ie l'euße semblablement volunties laißé aller auecq ses figures simples, s'il n'euß deu tuber qu'es mains des experts, & exercez en l'art, qui d'eux mesmes & à la simple veue de la figure eußent peu cognoistre & voir ce qui en est. Mais s'ay voulu seruir aux rudes & ignorans qui voudront en cognoistre quelque chose, & satisfaire à l'inslante poursuitte de mes bons seigneurs & amys, amateurs de cest Art, qui m'en ont a tant de fois requis & prié, qu'il ne m'a esté possible les esconduire, & m'exempter d'en mettre dehors quelque chose. En quoy veritablement i'ay esté d'autant plus hardy, qu'il me sembloit bien que l'experience que i'en ay faicte par long temps me deuoit auoir laißé quelque iugement & cognoißance pour en pouuoir parler à l'instruction & auancement des nouueaux & non experimentez en l'art, & au contentement des amys qui m'en ont si inslamment requis. Cest Art consiste en reigles & sections de lignes certaines, selon qu'il se pourra voir par ce qui est contenu en ce present œuure. Et se verra encores plus amplemont par le second œuure: auquel seront representées les figures de touts corps, mesmes des personnages, arbres, & paysages, pour entendre & cognoistre en quelle situation forme & grandeur ilz doiuent estre representez selon cest art: lequel œuure, auec l'ayde de Dieu, i'espere bien toll faire sortir en lumiere: si ie cognois ce mien premier labeur t'estre aggreable. Qui est ce que ie demande de toy pour touts recompence.          A Dieu.

A iij

Cousin: *Livre de Perspective*

Paris: Jehan le Royer, 1560

$7\frac{5}{8}'' \times 6\frac{3}{8}''$

## Liure de Perspectiue

P OVR autant que toutes chofes egualles, femblent moindres les vnes que les autres au pris qu'elles font ou plus proches, ou plus efloignees de noftre veüe : foit qu'elles foient viz à viz de nous, foit qu'elles foient pofees fus lignes Perpendiculaires à la ligne Horizontalle de noftre veüe, ou autrement. Aucuns ont e-fté d'aduiz, que les frontz des quarreaux d'vn paué eftants fus la ligne Terre, ou fus ligne Equidiftante à icelle, fe doiuent racourcir au perfonnage. Et femblablement que les Colomnes eftants au front d'vn baftiment, viz à viz de nous, deuoient eftre racourcies en Perfpectiue. En quoy ils f'abufent : car combien qu'il foit veritable que des Colomnes eftants au front d'vn baftiment viz à viz de nous, les plus prochaines femblent plus lôgues, & les plus lointaines plus courtes : fi ne f'enfuit il pourtant qu'il faille racourcir lefdittes Colomnes en Perfpectiue : pourtant qu'eftants faites egualles au Perfpectif mefmes, par mefme raifon (fur laquelle ils fe fondent) elles nous femblerôt inegualles & racourcies. Ce que vous entendrez plus clairement par la figure que ie vous prefente icy pour exemple. Car fi vous auiez en vn grand pan de mur fait peindre quantité de Colomnes egualles, telles qu'il vous plaira, côme vous en voyez icy fix, & les eufsiez faites eguallemêt efloignees les vnes des autres, vous eftât au meilieu d'i-celles, verriez le racourciffemêt defdittes Colomnes eftre naturellement donné, & ce fans artifice aucun. Dont f'enfuit que les Colomnes & Entrecolomnes plus efloignees vous fembleroient moindres, & les plus prochaines de vous, plus grandes, combien qu'ils foient egualles. Puis donc que naturellement ce qui eft viz à viz de vous fus la ligne Terre, fe racourcift, il n'eft befoin y adioufter racourciffement

5

# ANACREONTIS
*Teï antiquiſſimi poëtæ Lyrici*
*Odæ , ab Helia Andrea*
*Latinæ factæ.*

### DE LYRA.

ANTARE nunc A-
tridas,
Núc expeteſſo Cad
mum:
Teſtudo verò ner-
uis
Solum refert Amo-
rem.
Mutanda fila nuper
Curo, lyrámque totam.
Et Herculis labores
Mox ordior, ſed illa
Sonans refert Amores.

A.iij.

Anacreon

Paris: Robert Estienne and Guillaume Morel, 1556

$4\frac{3}{4}'' \times 2\frac{1}{2}''$

# Tumbeau de treshaul-

## TE, TRESPVISSANTE ET

### TRESCATHOLIQVE PRINCESSE

Madame Elisabeth de France,
Royne d'Espagne.

### EN PLVSIEVRS LANGVES.

*Recueilli de plusieurs sçauans personnages de la
France.*

NOLI ALTVM SAPERE SED TIME

## A PARIS,

*Par Robert Estienne Imprimeur du Roy.*

### M. D. LXIX.

*Tumbeau de Mme. Princesse Élisabeth*

Paris: R. Estienne, 1569

$7\frac{1}{2}'' \times 4''$

 X E M P L V M fidei vis non vulga-
re, Viator,
Noſſe triplex? vnu noueris hunc
tumulum:
In quo Silliacus Caſtrææ gloria
gentis,
Silliacóque fides contumulata iacet.
Vix ad bis denos trieterida iunxerat annos,
Et thalamis fuerat pacta marita nouis:
Impia cùm Gallos in bella vocaret Erinnys,
Próque piis pugnans fortiter ille cadit.
Sed dum ſemanimum iacet alta in ſtrage cadauer,
Annulus in digito fortè iugalis erat:
Quem prædo auellens violentiùs,excitat ipſo
E leto tenuis relliquias animæ.
Colligit has,& vim vitat prædonis auari,
Dum miſerans illum tollit amicus humo.
Sed mox deficiens ſocii portantibus vlnis
Immoritur,moriens tot tamen antè refert:
Hoc tibi commendo ſocialis pignus amoris,
Quod ſponſæ reddas dulcis amice meæ.
Dixerat,& vultu mortem meliore recepit,
Ter ſibi ſeruatam conſcius eſſe fidem.
Prima fides,animus Chriſto,Regi altera,corpus,
Annulus eſt ſponſæ tertia miſſa fides.

I. A V R A T V S  R E G I V S  P O E T A.
A.ij.

Dorat and Ronsard: *Épitaphes sur le duc de Montmorency*

Paris: Ph. de Roville, 1567

$7\frac{1}{8}'' \times 4''$

# SILLACII CASTRAEI

## BELLI MVSARVM'QVE MV-
### NERIBVS INSTRVCTISSIMI,
animi corporiſque dotibus ornatiſſimi, Tumu-
lus, variis Poëtarum inſcriptionibus inſignitus.

# Le Tũbeau du ſeigneur

## DE LA CHASTRE, DICT DE
### SILLAC, GENTIL-HOMME NAGVE-
res orné des excellences du corps & de l'eſprit,
& garni de la cognoiſſance des lettres & armes:
graué d'inſcriptions de diuers Poëtes.

### A PARIS,
*Par Robert Eſtienne Imprimeur du Roy.*
### M. D. LXIX.
# AVEC PRIVILEGE.

*Tumbeau du seigneur de la Chastre*

Paris: R. Estienne, 1569

$7'' \times 4''$

# C'EST L'ORDRE ET
FORME QVI A ESTE TENV AV
ſacre & couronnement de treſ-haute, treſ-excellen-
te, & treſ-puiſſante princeſſe Madame ELIZABET
d'Auſtriche Roine de France: faiⱦ en l'Egliſe de
l'Abbaie ſainⱦ Denis en France le vingt cinquieſme iour de Mars, *1571.*

*A PARIS,*

De l'Imprimerie de *Denis du Pré*, pour *Oliuier Codoré,*
rüe *Guillaume Ioſſe*, au *Heraut d'armes*, pres la rüe
*des Lombars.*

1  5  7  1.
AVEC PRIVILEGE DV ROY.

Ordre venu à la joyeuse entrée de Charles IX

Paris: Denys du Pré, 1571

$7\frac{1}{8}'' \times 4''$

# C'EST L'ORDRE ET

## FORME QVI A ESTE TENV AV

ſacre & couronnement de treſ-haute,treſ-excellen-
te,& treſ-puiſſante princeſſe Madame Elizabet
d'Auſtriche Roine de France: faiĉt en l'Egliſe de
l'Abbaie ſainĉt Denis en France le vingt cinquieſme iour de Mars, 1571.

Le Roy & la Roine eſtans le vingt
& troiſieſme iour dudiĉt mois de
Mars arriuez audiĉt ſainĉt Denis, le
vingt cinquieſme iour dudiĉt moïs
l'acte & ſolemnité dudiĉt ſacre fut
faiĉt ainſi qu'il ſ'enſuit.Il y auoit vn
gräd eſchauffault au milieu du cœur de ladiĉte Egliſe
aſſis droiĉt deuant le grand autel d'icelle,de la hauteur
de neuf piedz ou enuiron, aiant de longueur vingt
huiĉt piedz ſur vingt deux de large : eſtant lediĉt eſ-
chaffault garny de barrieres tout autour,fors à l'en-
droiĉt de l'eſcallier, par lequel lon y montoit, qui e-
ſtoit du coſté dudiĉt grand autel,& y auoit ſeize marches en hauteur, & puis ſe trouuoit vne eſpace d'enuiron ſix piedz de long, & auſſi large que lediĉt eſcallier. Et apres lon montoit vne autre marché pour en-
trer audiĉt grand eſchaffault.Enuiró le milieu duquel
tirant vn peu ſur le derriere y auoit vn hault dez de la
hauteur d'vn peu plus d'vn pied où lon mótoit deux
marches,lequel haut dez & marches qui contenoïét de

a ij

*Ordre venu à la joyeuse entrée de Charles IX*

Paris: Denys du Pré, 1571

$7\frac{5}{8}'' \times 4\frac{1}{8}''$

# Ornatiſsimi Cuiuſdam Viri, De Rebus Gallicis, Ad Staniſlaum Eluidium, Epiſtola.

**LVTETIÆ,**
*Apud Federicum Morellum Typo-*
*graphum Regium.*
1 5 7 3.
**CVM PRIVILEGIO REGIS.**

Pibrac: *De Rebus Gallicis*
Paris: Féderic Morel, 1573
$6\frac{3}{8}'' \times 3\frac{3}{4}''$

# AD SERENISSIMAM

## AC CHRISTIANIS s. REGINAM
### CATHARINAM MEDICAEAM
HENRICI III. Galliae & Poloniae
regis Chriſtianiſs.matrem,

GERMANI AVDEBERTI Aurelij
CARMEN.

*VI potius Regina potĕs, Regum-*
*que creatrix,*
*Quam tibi ſacrĕtur Verini car-*
*mina vatis*
*Syllanae veteres vrbis celebran-*
*tia cunas,*
*Illuſtreſque viros, totamque ab*
*origine prolem,*
*Maioreſque tuos? quorum tu maxima iure* ❧
*Gloria cenſeris: ſunt haec tibi propria dona*
*Magnanimum Heroum genus alta e ſtirpe trahenti,*
*Summoſque augenti Medicaeae gentis honores.*
*Nobilis vt fuluo decoratur gemma metallo,*
*Vt radijs magis illa ſuis illuminat aurum:*
*Sic ſplendente domo, & claris natalibus orta*
*Scintillas, raraque tuos virtute parentes*
*Illuſtras magis, atque magis : moderatio magno*
*Magna licet fuerit Coſmo, prudentia ſolers*

ă ij

Pietro Angelio de Barga: *Syriados liber*

Paris: Mamert Patisson, 1582

$8\frac{1}{2}'' \times 4\frac{5}{8}''$

# MARGVERITES

## DE LA MARGVERITE

### DES PRINCESSES,

#### TRESILLVSTRE

##### ROYNE

###### DE

## NAVARRE.

A LYON,
**PAR IEAN DE TOVRNES.**
M. D. XLVII.

*Auec Priuilege pour six ans.*

Marguerite de Navarre: *Marguerites de la Marguerite des princesses*

Lyons: Jean de Tournes, 1547

$5'' \times 2\frac{3}{4}''$

15

# LE MIROIR
## DE L'AME PECHE-
### RESSE.

Seigneur DIEV crée en moy cœur net.  Pſeau.50.

OV eſt l'Enfer remply entiere-
ment
De tout malheur, trauail, peine,
& tourment?
Ou eſt le puitz de malediction,
D'ou ſans fin ſort deſeſperation?
Eſt il de mal nul ſy profond abyſme,
Qui ſuffiſant fuſt pour punir la diſme
De mes pechés? qui ſont en ſy grand nombre,
Qu'infinité rend ſy obſcure l'ombre,
Que les compter, ne bien voir, ie ne puys:
Car trop auant auecques eux ie ſuis.
Et qui pis eſt, ie n'ay pas la puiſſance
D'auoir d'vn ſeul, au vray, la congnoiſſance.
Bien ſens en moy, que i en ay la racine,

Et au

Marguerite de Navarre: *Marguerites de la Marguerite des princesses*

Lyons: Jean de Tournes, 1547

$5\frac{1}{4}'' \times 3\frac{1}{4}''$

*Au moins vaincrons ayans ceste defenſe,*
*Encor' que nous ayons fait mainte offenſe,*
*Puis qu'à peché,ne nous ſommes donnez.*

F I N.

Oraiſon de l'Ame fidele, à ſon

SEIGNEVR DIEV.

*Eigneur,duquel le ſiege,ſont les Cieux;*
*Le marchepied, la terre, & ces bas*
*lieux ;*
*Qui en tes bras encloz le firmament,*
*Qui es touſiours nouueau,antique & vieux,*
*Rien n'eſt caché au regard de tes yeux;*
*Au fonds du roc tu vois le diamant,*
*Au fonds d'Enfer ton iuſte iugement,*
*Au fonds du ciel ta Maieſté reluire,*
*Au fonds du cœur le couuert penſement,*
*Qui eſt celuy qui te voudroit inſtruire?*
*Plus qu'vn eſclair ton œil eſt importable,*
*Plus qu'vn tonnerre eſt ta voix effrayable,*
*Plus qu'vn grand vent ton eſprit nous eſtonne,*
*Plus que fouldre eſt ton coup ineuitable,*

*Plus*

Marguerite de Navarre: *Marguerites de la Marguerite des princesses*

Lyons: Jean de Tournes, 1547

$5\frac{1}{4}'' \times 2\frac{7}{8}''$

# CHIROMAN-
## CE DE IOANNES
### INDAGINE.

### LIVRE PREMIER.

CHAPITRE I.

ES Grecz appellent Chiro-
mance, diuination qui est faite & cueillie par laspect & regard de la main:& si long temps
ha esté en vsage enuers les anciens, que ce mot Chiromance,
qui est tresancien,le dit & demonstre. Or ie qui
veux escrire les obseruations de cest art, pense
quil est necessaire premierement descrire & de-
noter celle main de lhomme, & declarer ses par-
ties: par lesquelles choses seront plus facilement
congnues les sentēces de Vaticination ou progno-
stiquer par linspection de la main qui cela demonstre. La main ouuerte,ainsi lappellerons, est
quand elle sera estendue & applanie : & linterieu-
re place de dedens, sappelle la Palme de la main:
au my

Ioannes de Indagine: *Chiromance*

Lyons: Jean de Tournes, 1549

$5\frac{1}{4}'' \times 2\frac{7}{8}''$

# Le priuilege du Roy.

**H**Enri *par la grace de Dieu Roy de Frã-*
*ce, A noz aymez & feaux Con-*
*seillers les gens tenans noz Courts de Parle-*
*ment à Paris, Tholouze, Rouen, Bourdeaux,*
*Dijon, Dauphiné & Prouence, Preuost de*
*Paris, Seneschal de Lyon, Bailly de Rouen, &*
*à tous noz autres Iusticiers & Officiers, ou*
*leurs Lieuxtenans, à chacun d'eux comme à*
*luy appartiendra, Salut & dilection. Noz*
*bien aymez Iaques de Strada Mantuan, & Thomas Guerin Marchand*
*Libraire demourant à Lyon, nous ont fait dire & remontrer que à grans*
*fraiz & despens ilz ont recouuert & dressé vn liure ainsi intitulé:*
Epitome Thesauri antiquitatũ. Hoc est, Imperatorum Romanorum
Orientalium & Occidentalium Iconum, ex antiquis Numismatibus
quàm fidelissimé deliniatarum. Ex Musæo Iacobi de Strada Man-
tuani Antiquarii &c. *Lequel liure lesdits de Strada & Guerin impri-*
*meroient voluntiers pour le bien commun de nostre Republique, illustra-*
*tion & intelligence des antiquitez & bonnes lettres, & contentement*
*des sauteurs & amateurs d'icelles, tant en Latin, François, Italien,*
*Allemand que Espaignol: mais ilz doutent qu'apres qu'ilz auront fait*
*les fraiz & employé grande somme de deniers pour la correction, pa-*
*pier & impression dudit liure, & pour la taille des figures qu'il conuien-*
*dra pour ce faire tailler & grauer, Autres Libraires & Imprimeurs*
*de nostre Royaume ne voulissent semblablement imprimer ou faire*
*imprimer, vendre & distribuer ledit liure contrefait souz leurs cor-*
*rections, & par ce moyen les frustrer de leurs labeurs, merites, fraiz*
*& despenses, s'il ne leur estoit par nous pourueu de noz grace &*
*remede conuenable, humblement requerant icelui. Parquoy nous ces*
*choses considerees desirans que ledit liure vienne en euidence, pour donner*
*aussi moyen ausdits de Strada & Guerin de recouurer le merite de leurs*
*labeurs & impenses, A iceux auons permis & ottroyé, permettons &*
*ottroy*

Strada: *Thesaurus Antiquitatum*

Lyons: Jean de Tournes, 1553

$7\frac{1}{8}'' \times 4\frac{1}{8}''$

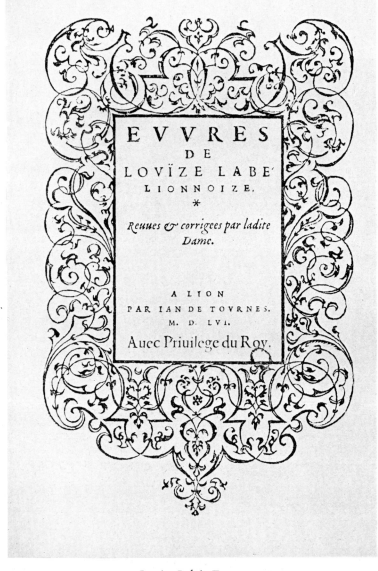

Louise Labé: *Euvres*

Lyons: Jean de Tournes, 1556

$5\frac{1}{4}'' \times 3\frac{1}{2}''$

# DEBAT DE FOLIE
## ET D'AMOVR,
### PAR
## LOVÏZE LABE'
#### LIONNOIZE.

### ARGVMENT.

IVPITER *faiſoit ⁊n grand feſtin, ou eſtoit cõman-
dé à tous les Dieus ſe trouuer. Amour ⁊ Folie arriuent
en meſme inſtant ſur la porte du Palais : laquelle eſtant ià
fermee, ⁊ n'ayant que le guichet ouuert, Folie ⁊oyant
Amour ià preſt à mettre ⁊n pied dedens, s'auance ⁊
paſſe la premiere. Amour ſe ⁊oyant pouſſé, entre en co-
lere : Folie ſoutient lui apartenir de paſſer deuant. Ils
entrent en diſpute ſur leurs puiſſances, dinitez ⁊ pré-
ſeances. Amour ne la pouuant ⁊eincre de paroles, met
la main à ſon arc, ⁊ lui laſche ⁊ne fleſche, mais en ⁊ain:
pource que Folie ſoudein ſe rend inuiſible: ⁊ ſe ⁊oulant
⁊enger, óte les yeus à Amour. Et pour couurir le lieu
ou ils eſtoient, lui mit ⁊n bandeau, fait de tel artifice,
qu'impoſſible eſt lui óter. Venus ſe pleint de Folie, Iupiter ⁊eut entendre leur diferent. Apolon ⁊ Mercure de-
baťet le droit de l'une ⁊ l'autre partie. Iupiter les ayant
longuement ouiz, en demande l'opinion aus Dieus : puis
prononce ſa ſentence.*

a 5

---

Louise Labé: *Euvres*

Lyons: Jean de Tournes, 1556

$5\frac{1}{4}'' \times 3''$

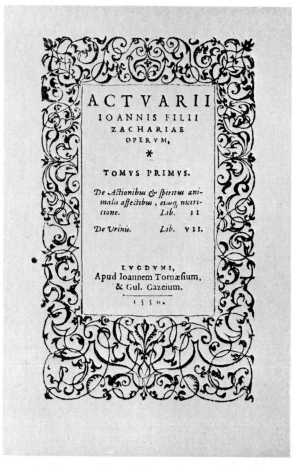

Ioannes Actuarius: *De actionibus et spiritus animalis affectibus*

Lyons: Jean de Tournes, 1556

$3\frac{3}{4}'' \times 2\frac{3}{8}''$

248

# Gaye Suetone Tranquile, de la
## VIE DE NERON CLAV-
### DE CESAR,
#### LIVRE VI.

**D** E L A race Domicie furent en bruit & eftime deus familles : celle des Caluins, & celle des Enobarbes. Les Enobarbes pour auteur de leur origine, enfemble de leur furnom, ont Luce Domice : au deuant duquel, ainfi que iadis il retournoit des champs, deus ieunes iouuenceaus de forme trefexcellente, [1] font dits s'eftre prefentez de rencôtre, & lui auoir commandé qu'il annonçaſt au Senat & au Peuple Rommein, [1] la victoire, dont lon eſtoit encore en doute : & pour aprobacion de leur [2] Mageſté lui auoir en forte froté doucement les ioues, qu'ils lui rendirent le poil de fa barbe, de noir, blond, & femblable à airein : laquelle marque demeura de mefme en fes fucceffeurs, fi que la plus part eurent la barbe blonde. Et ayans aminiſtrez fept Confulats, double Cenfure, uz deus trionfes, & faits de l'eſtat des Patrices, perſeuererent tous au mefme furnom, fans que point ils ufurpaſſent aucuns prenoms, fors de

1 Cette victoire contre les Tarquiniés & les Latins eſt amplement deſcrite par Tite Liue au fecond liure de la premiere Decade.

2 Qu'ils eſtoiét Dieus: car ils furent eſtimez Caſtor & Polux.

Suetonius: *De la vie des XII Césars*

Lyons: Jean de Tournes, 1556

$7\frac{1}{4}'' \times 4\frac{5}{8}''$

# A MONSIEVR

## DE LA RIVOIRE,

### SECRETAIRE DE

#### LA ROYNE DE

#### NAVARRE.

\*

 Oins ne pouuoit le deuoir mien
enuers votre si liberale bonté
affeccionnément deuot , que,
estant par voz continuels bene-
fices tant de fois reueillé , mon-
trer (sinon par condigne reeon-
noissance pour le peu de son pouuoir, aumoins
par juste marque de gratuité) combien il se sent
tous les jours augmenter & croitre l'obligacion
auec l'affeccion, qui vous demeurent à jamais re-
deuablement liez : mais d'autant liberalement,
que la bonne volonté se peut de soy en autrui li-
brement affeccionner. Aussi ay je toujours crù le
bienfait d'ami oublié estre plustot vn ingrat oubli

a　2　　　de

Ovid: *Métamorphoses*

Lyons: Jean de Tournes, 1557

$5\frac{1}{4}'' \times 3\frac{1}{8}''$

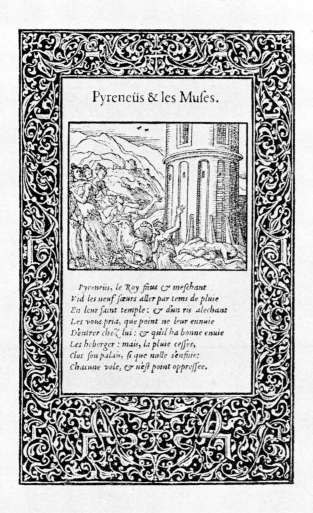

Ovid: *Métamorphoses*

Lyons: Jean de Tournes, 1557

$5\frac{1}{8}'' \times 3\frac{1}{4}''$

496

# LIBER ESTHER.

**CAPVT I.**

A IN diebus Aſſueri qui regnauit ab India vſq; Aethiopiam ſuper centum vigintiſeptem prouincias : quando ſedit in ſolio regni ſui: Suſan ciuitas regni eius exordium fuit. Tertio igitur anno imperij ſui fecit grande cōuiuium cunctis principibus , & pueris ſuis, fortiſſimis Perſarum, & Medorum inclytis, & præfectis prouinciarum coram ſe, vt oſtenderet diuitias gloriæ regni ſui, ac magnitudinem, atq; iactantiam potentiæ ſuæ, multo tēpore, centū videlicet & octoginta diebus. Cūq; implerentur dies conuiuij, inuitauit oēm populū qui inuentus eſt in Suſan à maximo vſq; ad minimum: & iuſſit ſeptem diebus conuiuiū præparati in veſtibulo horti, & nemoris , quod regio cultu & manu conſitū erat. Et pēdebant ex omni parte tētoria aërei coloris, & carbaſini ac hyacinthini, ſuſtētata funib?

B byſſinis, atq; purpureis q ebutneis cir-

culis inſerti erant, & colūnis marmoreis fulciebātur. Lectuli quoq; aurei & argētei, ſup pauimētū ſmaragdino & pario ſtratum lapide, diſpoſiti erāt: quod mira varietate pictura decorabat. Bibebāt autem qui inuitati erāt, aureis poculis, & aliis atq; aliis vaſis cibi inferebantur. Vinū quoq; vt magnificentia regia dignum erat, abundans & præcipuum ponebatur. Nec erat qui nolentes cogeret ad bibendū: ſed ſicut rex ſtatuerat, præponens menſis ſingulos de principibus ſuis, vt ſumeret vnuſquiſq; quod vellet. Vaſthi quoq; regina fecit conuiuiū feminarū in palatio, vbi rex Aſſuerus manere conſueuerat. Itaq; die ſeptimo, cū rex eſſet hilarior, & poſt nimiā potatiōe incaluiſſet mero, præcepit Mauman & Bazatha & Harbona & Bagatha & Abgatha & Zethar & Charchas, ſeptē eunuchis qui in cōſpectu eius miniſtrabāt, vt introduceret reginā Vaſthi corā rege, poſito ſup caput ei? diademate, vt oſtēderet cūctis populis & principibus pulchritudinem illius: erat ēm pulchra valde.

C

*Biblia Sacra*

Lyons: Jean de Tournes, 1558

$5\frac{5}{8}'' \times 3\frac{3}{4}''$

18

Volendo Mattheo moſtrare Gieſu eſſere quel
vero Meſſia da Dio per gli Profeti promeſ-
ſo : narra per ordine da Abrahamo in giu,
tutta la ſua naturale genealogia. Racconta
le ſpoſalizie di Maria e Gioſeffo, la cócez-
zione di Chriſto, mediante lo Spirito ſan-
to, e qualmente Gioſeffo, ammonitone da
l'Agnolo, s'accompagna Maria.  C A P.  I.

Luc 3.e
Gen. 21.a
Gen. 25.c
Gen. 29.f
Gen. 38.g
Ge. 46.a
1.Par.2.b
Rut 4.d
1.Sa. 6.a
2.Sa.11.f
1.reg.11.g
1.Par.3.b
2.Reg.29
2.Reg 8.f
2. Re.15.g
2.Paral.
27.c
2 Paral.
28.d
1. Re.2.d
2.Re.23.f.
24.25

I L Libro de l'origine di Gieſu A
chriſto, figliuol di Dauidde, figliuol d'Abrahamo. Abrahamo generò Iſahache. Iſahache
generò Giacobbe. Giacobbe ge-
nerò Giuda e'i ſuoi frategli. Giuda generò Fareſe, e Faramo di Thamara. Fareſe generò Eſromo. Eſromo generò Aramo. Aramo generò
Aminadabbe. Aminadabbe generò Nahaſone.
Nahaſone generò Salmone. Salmone generò
Boozo di Rachabbe. Boozo generò Obetthe di
Ruttha. Obetthe generò Gieſſe. Gieſſe generò
Dauidde, il Re. Dauidde Re generò Salomone,
di quella che era ſtata d'Uria. Salomone generò
Rhoboamo. Rhoboamo generò Abia. Abia B
generò Aſa. Aſa generò Gioſaphatte. Gioſa-

phatte

*Nuovo Testamento*

Lyons: Jean de Tournes, 1558

$4'' \times 2\frac{1}{2}''$

M

*Clément Marot*

Lyons: Jean de Tournes, 1558

$3\frac{5}{8}'' \times 2''$

Due breui e faciii trattati,
Il primo d'Arithmetica: l'altro di Geometria:
ne i quali si contengono alcune cose nuoue
piaceuoli e utili, si à gentilhuomini come ar=
tegiani. Del Sig. GIO. FRANCESCO
PEVERONE DI CVNEO.

IN LIONE
PER GIO. DI TOVRNES.
M. D. LVIII.
Con Priuilegio del Rè.

Cuneo: *Due Brevi*

Lyons: Jean de Tournes, 1558

$7\frac{1}{4}'' \times 4\frac{1}{2}''$

I

# ILLVSTRATIONE
## DE GLI EPITAFFI
### ET MEDAGLIE
#### ANTICHE,

\*

### DI M. GABRIEL SYMEONI
#### FIORENTINO.

S O N O alcuni di cosi fatta opinio-
ne, che credano che la nobilta &
virtu della venerabile antichita,
insieme con la necessaria cogni-
tione delle historie, non porti honore ne vtile alcuno à quelli, che
di cio si dilettano, o per loro
piacere particulare, o per farne
partecipi gli altri huomini amato-
ri delle cose nobilissime & gentili, stimando falsaméte co-
tale professione vile, & quasi comune & facile à tutte le
persone : Per il che volendo à questi tali rispondere, &
aprire loro la verita del fatto, ecco che io vengo à mettere
innanzi le parole di Cicerone nella quinta Actione contro
à Verre, doue ei dice:

Tutti gl'essempli che si trouano & veggono notati ne i
marmi, & scritti nelle historie antiche, piene di maesta & di
vecchiezza, hanno non so che autorità & forza di persua-
dere, & di fare cognoscere vna cosa vera : & oltre à questo

Cic. in Verrè:
Exempla ex
vetere memo
ria, &c.

a      arreca

Simeoni: *Illustrazione de gli Epitaffi*

Lyons: Jean de Tournes, 1558

$6\frac{1}{2}'' \times 4\frac{1}{2}''$

# CALENDIER
## HISTORIAL.

A LYON
PAR IAN DE TOVRNES.

M. D. LXIII.

*Calendier Historial*
Lyons: Jean de Tournes, 1563
$3\frac{5}{8}'' \times 2''$

## AV LECTEVR.

AVcvns de noftre temps fou-
loyent en leurs Almanachs &
Calendiers defcrire, outre les
Nouuelles & pleines Lunes &
fes Quartiers, la Pronoftication, tant en
general de l'eftat & qualité de l'an qui
court pour lors, qu'en particulier de
beaucoup de cités & prouinces, comme
ceux qui confiderent peu l'eternelle pro-
uidence & gouuernement de Dieu en
ces chofes inferieures, & moins depen-
dans d'icelle, attribuans quafi le tout aux
caufes fecondes & aux eftoilles. Dont le
plus fouuent viennent à dire chofes non
feulement contre toute pieté chreftien-
ne, mais aufsi eflongnees de toute verité,
ainfi que le demonftre affez ce qui fuc-
cede de leurs vaines & fauffes pronofti-
cations. Laiffant donques ces vaines cu-
riofités à part, nous auons voulu feulement adioufter aucunes chofes à l'Alma-
nach hiftorial dignes vrayement d'eftre
leuës de tous, lefquelles font à plufiéurs
incognues, encores que quafi de tous
foyent mifes és Calendiers, comme le

A 2                    Nomb

*Calendier Historial*

Lyons: Jean de Tournes, 1563

$3\frac{7}{8}'' \times 2''$

*Les Foires plus notables.*

### I A N V I E R.
1 3 Foire à Lyon, & dure quinze iours.

### F E V R I E R.
3 Foire à S.Germain des Prés lez Paris, &
dure huit iours francs.

5 Foire à Niort en Poiſtou.

1 7 Foire à Geneue, & dure dix iours.

2 4 Foire à Paris.

### M A R S.
1 5 F. à Francfort, & dure vingt iours.

1 8 Foire à Sens.

### A V R I L.
1 3 F. à Lyon, & dure quinze iours.

### M A Y.
6 F à Niort en Poiſtou.

8 F. à Troye en Champaigne.

1 1 F. à Geneue, & dure dix iours.

### I V I N.
9 F. à Zurſac, & dure vn iour.

2 4 F. à Straſbourg, & dure quinze iours.

### I V I L L E T.
4 F. à Augſbourg.

### A O V S T.
1 F. à Fontenay en Poiſtou.

*Calendier Historial*

Lyons: Jean de Tournes, 1563

$3\frac{5}{8}'' \times 2\frac{1}{8}''$

*L A*

# MAGNIFICA ET

TRIVMPHALE ENTRATA DEL CHRI.
stianiss. Re di Francia Henrico secondo di questo nome
fatta nella nobile & antiqua Città di Lyone à luy &
à la sua serenissima consorte Chaterina alli 21.
di Septemb. 1 5 4 8.

*Colla particulare descritione della Comedia che fece*
*recitare la Natione Fiorentina à richiesta di sua*
*Maesta Christianissima.*

IN LYONE, appresso *Gulielmo Rouillio.*

1 5 4 9.

Con Priuilegio.

*La Magnifica Entrata del re Henrico II*

Lyons: Rouillé, 1549

$7'' \times 4\frac{1}{8}''$

L PORTO COSI BENE
aconcio conteneua nel ſuo centro molti
Grippi, Paliſcalmi, Schiphi, Batelli & altri infiniti legni aquatili & maritimi, liquali erano parati per cõdurre ſua Mae
ſtà à piglar piacere ſu il fiume, ſopra il
quale ſi feceno infiniti giochi, & recreatione di ſpiriti tanto di
gioſtre, di cõbatti che d'altri paſſamenti di diuerſi inſtrumenti
di Muſica. Il primo di quei vaſſelli contenuti nel porto, era vn
gran Barcone tutto coperto d'vn ſolaio di tauole: nel mezzo del
quale fu edificato vna ſala lungha tredeci paſſi, largha ſei &
alta dodici. Verſo poppa era vna porta & verſo prora vn'altra, lequale erano à l'antiqua corniciate & pilaſtrate di pila
ſtri ch'vſciuano fuora del muro tre dita, come per tutto erano
i muri della ditta ſala. Fra i pilaſtri de mura erano di gran fineſtre àl'antiqua ſerrate di tele bianche incerate & dipinte di
Lune in creſcente & delle impreſe reale. Sopra i muri della ia
ditta Sala era vn trauamento, ilquale ſeruiua di ſolaio à vn
aſtraco chera à l'intorno il ditto trauamẽto. Di fuora era que
ſta ſala tutta roſſa ma d'vn colore cinabrio finiſsimo, li capitelli
de pilaſtri, le porte & le fineſtre erano dorati, in ricchiti di
teſte di Lioni, gigli, & bacinette ſimilmente dorati. Della parte di dentro era tappezzata di dommaſco bianco & nero &
per terra erano di tapeti d'Aleſsãdria. Il trauamẽto era depinto delle diuiſe & impreſe reale. Queſto trauamento ſi poteua
diſcendere perche gl'era attaccato à quattro corriole & diſcen
deuaſi per quattro groſſe corde di ſeta bianca & nera: & que
ſto fu coſi ordinato acio ſi teneſsi li ſopra la collatione parata
ſenza che niſſuno ſi poteſsi auedere chel ſeruiſsi ad altro che
per trauamento. Fuora la ditta Sala tutta intorno era circun

I 2

La Magnifica Entrata del re Henrico II

Lyons: Rouillé, 1549

$6\frac{7}{8}'' \times 4''$

# AD CHRISTIA-
## NISS· FRANCIAE REGEM
### HENRICVM II.

*Gulielmi Rouilly Epistola.*

EGES DII mortales, immortalitatem côsequi possunt duabus potissi- mum rationibus, literarū honore, & armorum glo- ria. Quæ duo æternitati parandę officia, vni olim Palladi mysticè attribu- ta, post paucos, sed maximos Principes Alexan drū, Cæsarē, & Carolū Magnū simul sic pręsti- tit, & ea excercuit felicissimæ memoriæ Rex Frâciscus pater tuus ( ô Rex Christianissime) vt consummādam armorum gloriam filio re- linquens, literarum honorem ad summum ex- tulerit. Tu verò vtrumque sic es amplexus, vt togatæ militiæ decus patri aliquatenus conce- dens, rerum bellicarum victorias, & triûphos persequaris, pari nixu iuxtà, atque successu. Quamobrem cùm huius vtriusque laudis me- moranda exempla ad te, supra cæteros omnes Christianos Principes referri debeant: hoc ip- sum volumen, quod illa continet, tibi dicādum iure statuimus. In quo illustrissimi quique ab

a 2

Strada: *Iconum Promptuarii*

Lyons: Rouillé, 1553

$7\frac{1}{4}'' \times 4\frac{1}{4}''$

D. MEM. S.

*PRIMA PARS*

PROMPTVARII ICONVM
INSIGNIORVM A' SECVLO
hominum, fubiectis eorum vitis, per com-
pendium ex probatifsimis autori-
bus defumptis.

IN VIRTVTE,     ET FORTVNA.

LVGDVNI, APVD GVLIEL.
MVM ROVILLIVM.
1553.
*Cum Priuilegio Regio, ad annos decem.*

Strada: *Iconum Promptuarii*

Lyons: Rouillé, 1553

$7\frac{3}{8}'' \times 4\frac{1}{4}''$

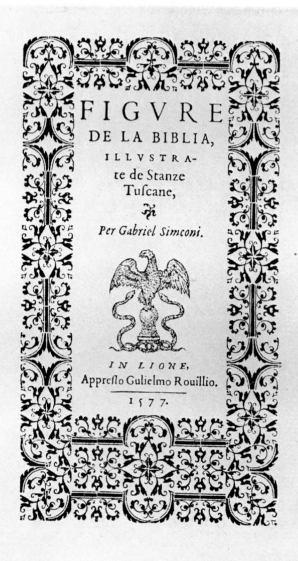

Simeoni: *Figure de la Biblia*

Lyons: Rouillé, 1577

$5\frac{3}{4}'' \times 3\frac{1}{8}''$

# ICONES
# HISTORIA
## RVM VETERIS
### TESTAMENTI,

*

Ad viuum expreſſæ, extremáque diligentia emendatiores
factæ, Gallicis in expoſitione homœoteleutis,
ac verſuum ordinibus (qui prius
turbati, ac impares) ſuo
numero reſtitutis.

MATVRA.

## LVGDVNI,
## Apud Ioannem Frellonium,
## 1547

Icones Veterum Historiarum Testamenti

Lyons: Frellon, 1547

$5\frac{1}{2}'' \times 3\frac{3}{8}''$

IONAS miſſus in Niniuen ad prædicandum, affligitur, quòd ſermo eius contra Niniuen non fuerit impletus.

IONAE    I.  II.  &  III.

Affligé fut par tempeſte ſoudaine
Ionas tranſmis en Niniue preſcher,
Trois iours au uentre il fut d'une Balaine,
Puis uers Niniue il ſe print à marcher.

N

*Icones Veterum Historiarum Testamenti*
Lyons: Frellon, 1547
$5\frac{1}{4}'' \times 3\frac{1}{2}''$

Erasmus: *Institutio Principis Christiani*

Basle: Froben, 1516

$6\frac{5}{8}'' \times 4\frac{1}{2}''$

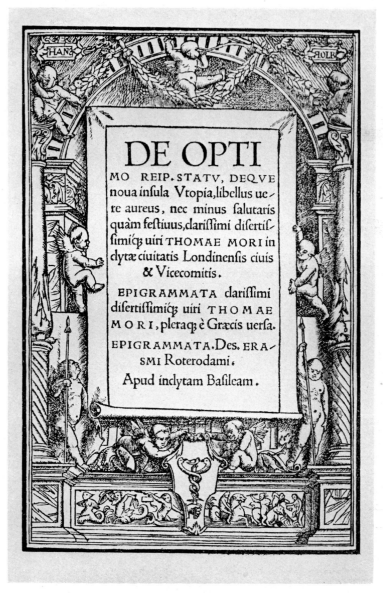

More: *De optimo Reipublicae Statu deque nova insula Utopia*

Basle: Froben, 1516

$7'' \times 4\frac{5}{8}''$

# ✢IOANNES FRO

BENIVS CANDIDO LE
CTORI S. D.

CCEPIMVS iam pridem, Erasmi Ro-
terodami compatris nostri Epigrammata à studiosis summopere flagita-
ri. Proinde dedimus operam, ut quicquid illius uersiculorum aut apud Bea
tum nostrum Rhenanum esset, aut Brunonem Amor-
bacchium, id omne uno complexi libello typis nostris
excuderemus. Quanquam intelligebamus, plurimum
nos hac re studiosis, Erasmo uero minimum gratifica-
turos. Nam magnam horum Epigrammatum partem
non in hoc scripsit ut æderentur, sed ut amiculis suis (ut
est minime morosus) obsequeretur. Quin ipsi uidimus
cum ab hinc sesquiannum apud nos ageret, Euangeli-
ca & Apostolica monumenta partim latine uertens,
partim recognoscens, & doctissimas illas in Nouū in-
strumentum Annotationes, nec non in diuum Hiero-
nymum scholia scriberet, deum immortalē, ꝗ laborio-
sis lucubrationibus, ꝗ pertinaci studio, quantum su-
doris illi cotidie exhauriebatur? Ipsi inquam uidimus,
non defuisse è magnatibus, qui uirum occupatissimū (si
quisquàm in literis unquam suit occupatus) interpella-

L 2     re de

Erasmus: *Epigrammata*

Basle: Froben, 1518

$5\frac{7}{8}'' \times 3\frac{3}{4}''$

N

**IO. FROBENIVS PIO**
**LECTORI S. D.**

DIVI Hilarij Pictauorū epi
scopi lucubrationes per Erasmū
Roterodamum nō mediocribus
sudoribus emendatas, formulis
nostris, operaꝗ nostra, quantum
licuit, ornauimus. Priorē æditio
nem nō damnamus, sed quid in
tersit, ipse cognosces ex collatio
ne, lector optime. simulꝗ uale
bis. Catalogum reperies in proxi
ma pagella.

In officinâ Frobeniana apud
inclytam Basileam, Anno. M.D.
XXIII. mense Febr.

DIONYSIVS

CLEOPATRA.

Hilarius: *Lucubrationes*

Basle: Froben, 1523

$9\frac{5}{8}'' \times 6\frac{1}{2}''$

# C· IVLII SOLINI PO

## LYHISTOR, RERVM TOTO

### ORBE MEMORABILIVM THE⸗
faurus locupletifsimus.

HVIC OB ARGVMENTI SIMILITVDINEM

## POMPONII MELAE DE SITV ORBIS

### LIBROS TRES, FIDE DILIGENTIAQVE
*fumma denuò iam recognitos, adiunximus.*

His accefferunt præter priora fcholia & tabulas geographicas permultas, PETRI quoq; OLIVARII Valentini, uiri in Geographia excellenter docti, annotationes, qui bus & loci non pauci, à plerifq; parum hactenus intellecti, dilucidè illuftrantur, & ne⸗ tuftis locorum appellationibus recentiora figillatim nomina fubijciuntur.

*Cum gemino Indice, quorum alter fupra res alias memorabiles, locorum ac re⸗
gionum omnium, marium ac finuum nomina, alter uerò recen⸗
tiores eorundem appellationes complectitur.*

PALMA ISING

BASILEAE, APVD MICH. ISIN⸗
GRINIVM, M. D. XLIII.

Solinus: *Rerum Toto Orbe Memorabilium Thesaurus*

Basle: Michel Isingrinius, 1543

$8\frac{1}{4}'' \times 5\frac{1}{8}''$

A

# TIBERIVS ET
## GAIVS GRACCI.

B

C INSI donc estant l'histoire des deux Grecs exposee, il reste que
nous escriuions aussi celle des deux Romains, en laquelle nous ne
verrons pas de moindres inconueniens aduenus à Tiberius & à
Gaius, qui tous deux furent fils de Tiberius Graccus : lequel encore qu'il eust esté deux fois Consul, & vne fois Censeur, & qu'il
eust eu l'honneur de deux triomphes, auoit neantmoins plus de
dignité & plus de gloire à cause de sa vertu seule, pour laquelle il
fut estimé digne d'espouser Cornelia fille de Scipió, qui desfit Annibal apres la mort
du pere : combien que de son viuant il ne luy eust point esté amy, ains plustost aduer-
saire & ennemy. On dit, qu'il trouua vn iour dedans son lict vne couple de serpens, &
D que les deuins ayans consideré que vouloit signifier ce presage, luy defendirent de
les tuer tous deux, & de les laisser aussi eschapper tous deux, mais ouy bien l'vn seule-
ment, luy asseurans que s'il faisoit mourir le masle, cela luy apporteroit la mort à luy-
mesme, & s'il tuoit la femelle, que ce seroit à Cornelia. Tiberius donc aimant sa femme, ioint qu'il estimoit estre plus raisonnable que luy mourust premier qu'elle, atten-
du qu'il estoit le plus vieil, & elle encore ieune, tua le masle, & laissa eschapper la femelle : mais il mourut tantost apres, laissant douze enfans viuans, lesquels il auoit
tous eus de Cornelia, laquelle apres le trespas de son mary, prenant tout le soin de sa
maison & de ses enfans, se monstra si honeste, si bonne enuers ses enfans, & si magna
nime, qu'on iugea Tiberius auoir sagement fait, d'auoir voulu mourir plustost que
E vne telle femme. Car estant en sa viduité, le Roy Ptolemæus luy voulut communiquer l'honneur du diademe royal, & la faire Royne, la demandant à femme : mais elle le refusa, & perdit en sa viduité tous ses enfans, exceptee vne fille, qu'elle donna en
mariage au ieune Scipion Africain, & Tiberius & Gaius dont nous escriuons presen-
tement, lesquels elle nourrit & institua si diligemment, qu'estans deuenus plus hone
stes & mieux conditionnez que nuls autres ieunes hommes Romains de leur temps,
on estima que la nourriture en valoit mieux que la nature : mais tout ainsi qu'és ima-
ges de Castor & de Pollux on apperçoit ne scay quoy de difference, qui fait cognoistre, que l'vn valoit mieux à la lucte & l'autre à la course : aussi entre ces deux ieunes
freres, parmy les autres grandes similitudes qu'ils auoyent, d'estre tous deux heureusement nez à la prouësse de leurs personnes, à la temperance, à la liberalité, aux lettres

Plutarch: *Les Vies*

Lausanne: Le Preux, 1574

$12\frac{3}{8}'' \times 6\frac{3}{4}''$

OBSERVATIONVM,

# QVÆ AD VETEREM
## Nuptiarum ritum
### pertinent,
## Liber singularis.

*Authore Ä. Hotomano Iurisconsulto & Aduocato in supremo senatu Parisiensi.*

Excudebat Ioannes le Preux

M. D. LXXXV

---

A. Hotman: *Observationum quae ad veterem Nuptiarum ritum pertinent*

Lausanne: Le Preux, 1585

$4\frac{7}{8}'' \times 2\frac{7}{8}''$

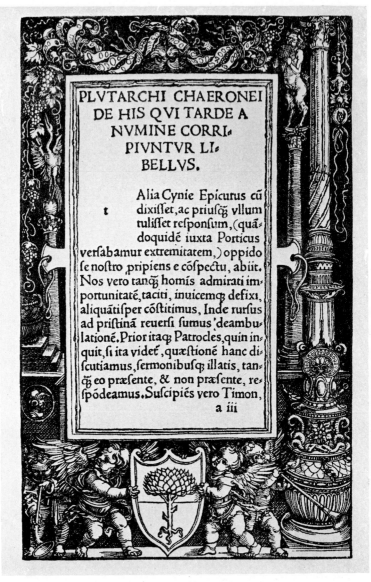

Plutarch: *De Sera Numinis Vindicta*

Nuremberg: Peypus, 1513

$7\frac{1}{2}'' \times 4\frac{3}{4}''$

# ❧ CL· PTOLOMAEI ☙

PHELVDIENSIS ALEXANDRI-
NI PHILOSOPHI ET MATHEMATICI
excellentiſſimi Phænomena, ſtellarum MXXII. fixarum
ad hanc ætatem reducta, atque ſeorſum in ſtudioſo-
rum gratiam·

Nunc primum edita, Interprete
Georgio Trapezuntio.

¶ Adiecta eſt iſagoge IOANNIS Nouiomagi ad ſtellarum
inerrantium longitudines ac latitudines, cui etiam acceſſere
Imagines ſphæræ barbaricæ duodequinquaginta.
ALBERTI DVRERI.

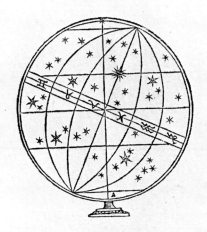

¶ Excuſum Coloniæ Agrippinæ, Anno M. D. XXXVII.
octauo Calendas Septembres.

Ptolomaeus: *Phaenomena*

Cologne: Anon, 1537

$7\frac{5}{8}'' \times 5''$

Hadriani Barlandi

# HOLLANDIÆ
## COMITVM HISTORIA
### ET ICONES:

*Cum selectis scholijs ad Lectoris lucem.*

*Eiusdem Barlandi*
Caroli Burgundiæ Ducis vita.

*ITEM*

VLTRAIECTENSIVM EPISCO.
porum Catalogus & res gestæ.

*Eiusdem argumenti libellus* GERARDO
NOVIOMAGO *auctore.*

FRANCOFVRTI
Apud Io. Wechelum, impensis Sigis. Feyerabend.

MDLXXXV.

Barlandus: *Hollandiae Comitum Historia*
Frankfurt: Wechel and Feyerabend, 1585
$5\frac{1}{4}'' \times 2\frac{3}{8}''$

I

# HADRIANI BAR-
LANDI DE REBVS GE-
STIS COMITVM HOLLAN-
DIÆ LIBELLVS.

De Theodorico I. Holl. Comite.
CAPVT I.

*AROLVS cogno-
mento Caluus, Ro-
manus Imperator,
& Galliarum Rex,
filius Ludouici Pij Cæsaris,
quum audiſſet Hollandiam
Imperatoriam terram à Da-
nis, qui Traiectum incolebăt,
vi bellica fœdari, ★ Ioannis o-
ctaui Pontificis rogatu, Prin-*

★ *Ioannes octa-
uus Pontifex, à
quo Carolus et-
iam Caluus in-
unctus memo-
ratur.*

a

Barlandus: *Hollandiae Comitum Historia*

Frankfurt: Wechel and Feyerabend, 1585

$4\frac{7}{8}'' \times 3''$

N. Taurellus: *Carmina Funebria*

Nuremberg: Gerlach, 1592

$5\frac{3}{8}'' \times 2\frac{7}{8}''$

# RITVS ECCLE-
## SIASTICI AVGVSTENSIS
EPISCOPATVS, TRIBVS PARTI-
bus fiue libris comprehenfi, nuncque
primum recogniti, editi atque
promulgati.

*AVCTORITATE REVE-*
*rendiß. & Illuſtriß. in Chriſto Patris ac*
*Domini* D. MARQVARDI Epi-
*ſcopi Auguſtenſis, & Præpo-*
*ſiti Bambergenſis.*

**DILINGÆ**
Excudebat Ioannes Mayer.

**M. D. LXXX.**

*Ritus Ecclesiae Augustensis*
Dillingen: Johann Mayer, 1580
$6\frac{3}{8}'' \times 4\frac{5}{8}''$

# MARQVARDVS DEI
## GRATIÁ EPISCOPVS AV-
### GVSTANVS, ET PRAEPOSI-
#### TVS BAMBERGENSIS,

Vniuerſo noſtro Clero Auguſtano ſa-
lutem in Domino.

*SAPIENTIBVS IL-
lis Architectis qui nouæ domus Dei, hoc eſt, Eccleſiæ ſan-
ctæ fundamenta iecerunt, &
iacta prouexerunt, adeoque ſo-
lidarunt, vt eadem domus aduerſus quoſlibet ven-
torum impetus firma & immota vſque perſiſtat,
citra omnem dubitationem fuit electum illud vas
Paulus Apoſtolus. Ad quam Apoſtolicam fa-
bricam bene conſeruandam, cùm alia multa con-
ferunt, tum ingens momentum habet vnitas illa
ſpiritus ab eodem Apoſtolo toties prædicata, &
quæ conſociandis, ac velut in eadem Repub. con-*

✠ ij          *tinendis*

*Ritus Ecclesiae Augustensis*
Dillingen: Johann Mayer, 1580
6″ × 4¼″

HADRIANI
IVNII MEDICI
EMBLEMATA,
AD
D. ARNOLDVM COBELIVM.

EIVSDEM
AENIGMATVM LIBELLVS,
AD
D. ARNOLDVM ROSENBERGVM.

ANTVERPIÆ,
Ex officina Christophori Plantini.
M. D. LXV.
CVM PRIVILEGIO.

Junius : *Emblemata*
Antwerp: Plantin, 1565
$5\frac{1}{2}'' \times 3\frac{3}{8}''$

# EXERCITATIO
## GRAMMATICA
### IN PSALMVM XXXIII.

Secundùm Hebræos  XXXIIII.

ROBERTO BELLARMINO
Politiano è Societate IESV
S. R. Ecclef. Presbyt.
Cardin. Auctore.

LVTETIÆ.

Ex officina GVLIELMI LEBE', in angulo
viarum S. Iohannis Bellouacenfis
& Lateranenfis.

M. DC. IX.

Bellarmine: *Grammaire Hébreu*

Paris: Guillaume Le Bé, 1609

$6\frac{3}{4}'' \times 3\frac{7}{8}''$

# DE IMITATIONE CHRISTI

## LIBER PRIMVS.

Admonitiones ad ſpiritualem vitam vtiles.

### CAPVT I.

*De imitatione Chriſti, & contemptu omnium vanitatum mundi.*

QVI ſequitur me, non ambulat in tenebris: dicit Dominus. Hæc ſunt verba Chriſti, quibus admonemur, quatenus vitam

A

Kempis: *De Imitatione Christi*

Paris: Imprimerie Royale, 1642

$10\frac{3}{8}'' \times 5\frac{7}{8}''$

# AV ROY.

IRE,

*Ie ne preſente pas à Voſtre Ma-
ieſté des terres étrangeres, & de
nouueaux mondes, quand ie luy
offre l'Empire de Conſtantinople,
puiſque c'eſt vn Trône ſur lequel
la valeur & la vertu ont éleué
vos Ayeux, & que celuy que vous
poſſedez vous donne des titres ſi*

ã iij

G. de Ville-Hardouin: *Histoire de l'empire de Constantinople*

Paris: Imprimerie Royale, 1657

$11'' \times 5\frac{3}{8}''$

Les Saintes

# Métamorphoses,

OV

## Les Changemens

miraculeux de quelques grands Saints.

tirez de leurs vies,

Par J. Baudoin.

A PARIS,

En l'Imprimerie des nouueaux Caracthe-
res de P. Moreau, M.ᵉ Escriuain Juré
à Paris, & Imprimeur ord.ᵣᵉ du Roy,
Et se vend en la boutique au Palais, à la
Salle Dauphine, Par F. Rouuelin,
à l'Enseigne de la Verité. 1644.
Auec approb. des Doct. & priuil. du Roy.

Baudoin: *Les Saintes Métamorphoses*

Paris: Pierre Moreau, 1644

$6\frac{3}{4}'' \times 4\frac{1}{2}''$

424 Les saintes Metamorph.

deuoir de souffrir pour la gloire
de Jesus-Christ; nous ne deuons
point nous rebuter, ny du mépris
que font de nous les Méchans, ny
*Act.* des opprobres que nous endurons
*14.* „ en cette vie, puis qu'il faut que par
„ plusieurs tribulations nous entrions
„ dans le Royaume de Dieu.

Fin du douziéme & dernier
Discours.

Baudoin: *Les Saintes Métamorphoses*

Paris: Pierre Moreau, 1644

$6'' \times 4\frac{5}{8}''$

I

# ORDONNANCE
## DE
## LOVIS XIV·
### ROY DE FRANCE,
### ET DE NAVARRE.

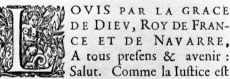

OVIS PAR LA GRACE DE DIEV, ROY DE FRAN-CE ET DE NAVARRE, A tous prefens & avenir : Salut. Comme la Iuftice eft le plus folide fondement de la durée des Eftats, qu'elle affure le repos des familles, & le bonheur des peuples; Nous avons employé tous nos foins pour la rétablir par l'autorité des Loix au dedans de noftre

A

*Ordonnance de Louis XIV*

Paris: Mettayer, 1667

$6\frac{5}{8}'' \times 4\frac{1}{4}''$

## AUTRE MEDAILLE
### SUR LA NAISSANCE DU ROY.

COMME les Romains ont eû foin de frapper des Médailles, pour perpétuer dans tous les fiécles le fouvenir de la conftellation, fous laquelle l'Empereur Augufte eftoit né ; on a voulu de mefme, fans rien donner aux chiméres de l'Aftrologie, tranfmettre à la poftérité la mémoire de la pofition, où fe trouvoit le Ciel dans le moment que Dieu dorna à la France le Prince, qui la rend la plus floriffante Monarchie du monde.

C'eft le fujet de cette Médaille. On a placé tout au tour les douze Signes, & les fept Planetes, dans la mefme pofition, où ils eftoient au moment de cette heureufe naiffance ; & fuivant l'idée de la Devife du Roy, dont le Soleil eft le corps, on a repréfenté au milieu la naiffance de ce Prince, par la figure du Soleil, qui fe leve. Le Roy enfant eft affis fur un Char élevé au deffus des nuës, & tiré par quatre chevaux. Le Char eft mené par la Victoire, qui d'une main luy montre une Couronne de laurier, fymbole des avantages, qu'il doit remporter fur les Ennemis de la France ; & qui de l'autre main tient les guides de fes Chevaux, comme pour l'affeurer qu'elle le conduira dans toutes fes entreprifes. Les mots de la Légende, ORTUS SOLIS GALLICI, fignifient, le lever du Soleil de la France. Ceux de l'Exergue, SEPTEMBRIS QUINTO, MINUTIS TRIGINTA OCTO ANTE MERIDIEM. M. DC. XXXVIII. veulent dire, le Roy né le 5 de Septembre, trente-huit minutes avant midy 1638.

*Médailles sur les évènements du règne Louis XIV*
Paris: Imprimerie Royale, 1702
$12\frac{5}{8}'' \times 8\frac{3}{8}''$

# LE POËME

## DE FONTENOY,

### NEUVIEME EDITION,

*Avec le Plan de la Bataille, l'Epître Dédicatoire au Roy, le Difcours préliminaire, des Notes, & autres Pieces.*

## A PARIS,

Chez PRAULT pere, Quai de Gévres, au Paradis.

## M. DCC. XLV.

*Avec Approbation & Permiſſion.*

Panckoucke: *Le Poème de Fontenoy*

Paris: Prault père, 1745

$5\frac{1}{2}'' \times 3\frac{7}{8}''$

# DIALOGUE

### SUR

## *LE MARIAGE*

## DE MADEMOISELLE GUERIN,

#### *AVEC*

## MONSIEUR DELATOUR.

### *L'HYMEN ET L'AMOUR.*

#### L'HYMEN.

 ERROIS-JE enfin combler ma plus douce esperance?
Et seroit-ce L'AMOUR qui paroit en ces lieux?
L'HYMEN depuis long-tems gémit de ton absence :
Mais pourquoi n'as-tu plus de bandeau sur les yeux?

#### L'AMOUR.

HYMEN, si mon bandeau m'est souvent nécessaire,
Ce n'est pas en ce jour, où la Raison m'éclaire ;
Ou de mille Vertus GUERIN & DELATOUR
Présentent le Tableau le plus cher à L'AMOUR.

Dialogue sur le Mariage Guérin et de la Tour

Paris: Guérin, 1745

$7\frac{7}{8}'' \times 5\frac{1}{8}''$

# STEPH. FABRETTI

## URBINATIS

*E SOCIETATE JESU PRESBITERI*

## LYRICA

E T

## EPISTOLÆ.

*LUGDUNI,*

Sumptibus FRATRUM DUPLAIN.

M. DCC. XLVII.
*CUM PRIVILEGIO REGIS:*

S. Fabretti: *Lyrica et Epistolæ*
Lyons: Duplain, 1747
$5\frac{1}{2}'' \times 3\frac{3}{8}''$

( 3 )

# DISCOURS

## SUR

## CE SUJET:

*Aſſigner les cauſes des Crimes, & donner les moyens de les rendre plus rares & moins funeſtes.*

*..... Cauſa latet, vis eſt notiſſima.*
O V I D E.

**I**L s'en faut bien que la Philoſophie ait embraſſe dans ſes progrès tous les objets, qu'il lui appartient d'éclairer & de réformer. Il s'en faut bien ſur-tout que nous ayons atteint dans la légiſlation criminelle cette perfection, qui eſt peut-être pour
A ij

*Mémoire sur les crimes*
Paris: Le Breton, 1754
$5\frac{3}{8}'' \times 2\frac{7}{8}''$

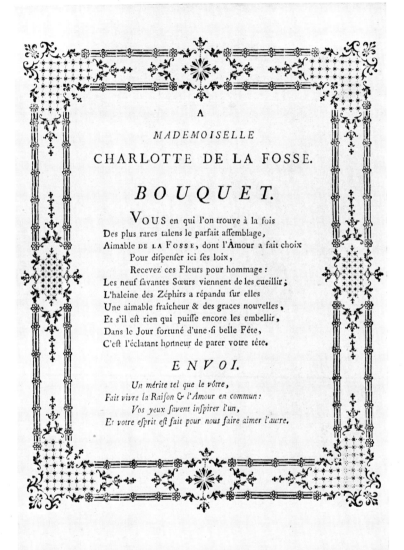

A

*MADEMOISELLE*

CHARLOTTE DE LA FOSSE.

# BOUQUET.

VOUS en qui l'on trouve à la fois
Des plus rares talens le parfait affemblage,
Aimable DE LA FOSSE, dont l'Amour a fait choix
    Pour difpenfer ici fes loix,
    Recevez ces Fleurs pour hommage :
Les neuf favantes Sœurs viennent de les cueillir ;
L'haleine des Zéphirs a répandu fur elles
Une aimable fraîcheur & des graces nouvelles,
Et s'il eft rien qui puiffe encore les embellir,
Dans le Jour fortuné d'une ·fi belle Fête,
C'eft l'éclatant honneur de parer votre tête.

## ENVOI.

*Un mérite tel que le vôtre,*
*Fait vivre la Raifon & l'Amour en commun :*
    *Vos yeux favent infpirer l'un,*
*Et votre efprit eft fait pour nous faire aimer l'autre.*

*Bouquet à Charlotte de la Fosse*

Paris: Anon, 1754

$6\frac{5}{8}'' \times 5\frac{1}{4}''$

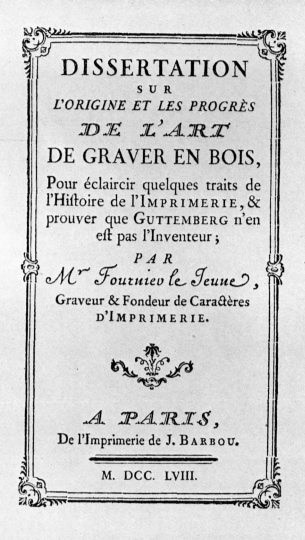

P. S. Fournier: *Dissertations, etc.*

Paris: Barbou, 1758–66

$5\frac{1}{4}'' \times 3''$

# DISSERTATION

*S U R*

## L'ORIGINE ET LES PROGRÈS

*D E  L'A R T*

### DE GRAVER EN BOIS,

*Pour éclaircir quelques traits de l'Histoire
de l'IMPRIMERIE, & prouver
que GUTTEMBERG n'en est pas
l'Inventeur.*

D<small>E S</small> erreurs foûtenues par des Au-
teurs célèbres, & long-temps accré-
ditées, font de nature à en impofer:
elles ont tenu & ne tiennent encore
que trop fouvent la vérité captive.
C'eft une erreur de cette efpèce qui
me paroît avoir fait donner à Gut-

A ij

P. S. Fournier: *Dissertations, etc.*

Paris: Barbou, 1758–66

$5\frac{1}{4}'' \times 3''$

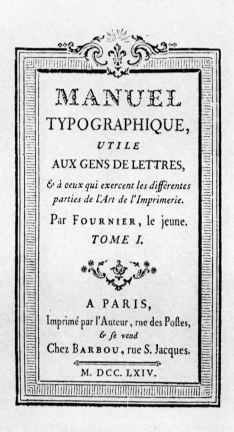

P. S. Fournier: *Dissertations, etc.*

Paris: Barbou, 1758-66

$4\frac{1}{4}'' \times 2\frac{3}{8}''$

# AVERTISSEMENT
## PRÉLIMINAIRE.

Pour rendre cet Ouvrage plus inté-
reſſant aux yeux des GENS DE LETTRES,
& pour remplir en même temps la partie qui les regarde, annoncée par le titre,
je donne dans ce ſecond Volume un
exemple des différents caractères qui
ſont ordinairement d'uſage dans l'Imprimerie, ſans oublier aucune des nuances qui ſervent à les faire diſtinguer.

Cette partie de l'Art Typographique, qui entre dans l'ordre des con-
noiſſances analogues à celles des gens
de Lettres, eſt communément fort né-

P. S. Fournier: *Dissertations, etc.*

Paris: Barbou, 1758–66

$4\frac{1}{4}'' \times 2\frac{3}{8}''$

# MANUEL TYPOGRAPHIQUE.

## PREMIÈRE PARTIE.

## LA GRAVURE,
### OU TAILLE DES POINÇONS.

Pour être un bon Graveur de Caractères, il faut être Typographe, c'eſt-à-dire, ſavoir tous les détails du méchaniſme de la Fonderie & de l'Imprimerie, afin d'y aſſujétir ſon travail. Maître de l'art, le Graveur doit tout prévoir dans la fonte & dans l'impreſſion. C'eſt par-là que les Simon de Colines, les Garamond, les

A

P. S. Fournier: *Dissertations, etc.*

Paris: Barbou, 1758–66

$4\frac{1}{4}'' \times 2\frac{3}{8}''$

308

# OFFICE

## POUR TOUTES LES FÊTES

### *DE LA* S<sup>te</sup> *VIERGE,*

#### QUI N'ONT PAS D'OFFICE PROPRE.

##### *A MATINES.*

Notre Pere, &c.

Je vous falue, Marie, &c.

Je crois en Dieu, &c.

**S**EIGNEUR, ouvrez mes levres, ℟. Et ma bouche annoncera vos louanges. *Pf.* 50 : 16.

Mon Dieu, venez à mon aide,

℟. Seigneur, hâtez-vous de me fecourir. *Pf.* 69. 1.

Gloire au Pere, au Fils & au Saint-Efprit ; comme elle étoit au commencement, qu'elle foit à préfent & toujours & dans les fiecles des fiecles. Ainfi foit-il. Louez le Seigneur.

*Invitatoire.* Venez, adorons Jefus - Chrift qui eft né de la Vierge Marie. *Math.* 1 : 16.

###### HYMNE.

**Q**Ue votre gloire eft éclatante, ô Vierge iffue de la race de David ! Vous êtes élevée dans le Ciel fur un trône fublime au-deffus de toutes les puiffances céleftes.

C'eft vous qui devenant mere, fans perdre l'honneur de la virginité, avez préparé dans votre fein un augufte fanctuaire au Roi de l'Univers. C'eft de vous que

*Office Divin*

Sens: Tarbé, 1763

$5\frac{1}{2}'' \times 3\frac{1}{4}''$

# ORDONNANCE
## DU ROI,
*Pour régler l'EXERCICE*
*de l'Infanterie.*

### Du 1.er Janvier 1766.

## DE PAR LE ROI.

A MAJESTÉ jugeant à propos de faire quelques changemens à l'Exercice de l'Infanterie, qu'Elle avoit réglé par son Ordonnance du 20 mars 1764, pour réduire les manœuvres & l'Exercice aux mouvemens les plus simples, Elle a ordonné & ordonne ce qui suit :

A

*Ordonnance sur l'infanterie*

Paris: Imprimerie Royale, 1766

$7\frac{3}{4}'' \times 4\frac{3}{4}''$

# COMPTE

## *RENDU AU ROI,*

Par M. NECKER,

Directeur général des Finances.

*Au mois de Janvier 1781.*

Imprimé par ordre de SA MAJESTÉ.

A PARIS,

DE L'IMPRIMERIE ROYALE.

M. D CC LXXXI.

*Compte rendu de M. Necker*

Paris: Imprimerie Royale, 1781

$7\frac{1}{8}'' \times 4\frac{3}{4}''$

P

# ÉLOGE
## *DU MARÉCHAL*
# DE CATINAT.

 ANS cette foule de Génies célèbres
en tout genre, que la Nature sembloit
avoir de loin préparés & mûris, pour
en faire l'ornement d'un seul règne,
l'orgueil de nos annales & l'admiration du monde;
dans ce siècle resplendissant de gloire, dont tous
les rayons viennent se confondre & se réunir au
trône de Louis XIV, j'observe avec étonnement
un homme qui prenant sa place au milieu de tous
ces grands hommes, sans avoir rien qui leur res-
semble, & sans être effacé par aucun d'eux, forme
seul avec tout son siècle un contraste frappant,
digne de l'attention des Sages & des regards de
la Postérité. Placé dans une époque & chez une

A iij

de la Harpe: *Éloge de M. Catinat*

Paris: Demonville, 1775

$6\frac{1}{8}'' \times 3\frac{5}{8}''$

# CONSEILS

## UN JEUNE POETE.

### P I E C E

## QUI A REMPORTE LE PRIX
de l'Académie Françoise, en 1775.

*Par M.* DE LA HARPE.

---

*Doctrina fed vim promovet infitam.* HOR.

---

*A PARIS*,

Chez DEMONVILLE, Imprimeur-Libraire de l'Académie
Françoise, rue S. Severin, aux Armes de Dombes.

M. D C C. L X X V.

de la Harpe: *Conseils*

Paris: Demonville, 1775

$6\frac{1}{4}'' \times 3\frac{5}{8}''$

# JEANNE GRAY,

## ANECDOTE

## ANGLOISE.

### PAR M. D'USSIEUX.

## A PARIS,

Chez B R U N E T, Libraire, rue des Ecrivains.

## M. D C C. L X X V I.

d'Ussieux: *Jeanne Gray*

Paris: Brunet, 1776

$5\frac{5}{8}'' \times 3\frac{1}{8}''$

# ELIZENE,
## ANECDOTE OTTOMANE.

LE mois le plus riant de l'année pour le peuple de Conſtantinople, c'eſt-à-dire, le mois d'Avril, venoit de renaître, & le Serrail du Grand-Seigneur s'apprêtoit à célébrer, avec tout le faſte ordinaire aux Orientaux, cette fête annuelle

*Tome I.*             S

d'Ussieux: *Le Décaméron François*

Paris: Nyon, 1783

$5\frac{3}{8}'' \times 3\frac{5}{8}''$

# LA
# FOLLE JOURNÉE,

## OU

## LE MARIAGE DE FIGARO,

### COMÉDIE

### EN CINQ ACTES, EN PROSE.

PAR M. DE BEAUMARCHAIS.

*Repréfentée pour la première fois, par les Comédiens
français ordinaires du Roi, le mardi 27 avril 1784.*

En faveur du badinage,
Faites grace à la raifon. *Vaud. de la pièce.*

DE L'IMPRIMERIE DE LA SOCIÉTÉ LITTÉRAIRE-
TYPOGRAPHIQUE;

*Et fe trouve à Paris,*

Chez RUAULT, libraire, au Palais-Royal, près
le théâtre, n° 216.

1 7 8 5.

Beaumarchais: *La Folle Journée*
Paris: Société littéraire, 1785
$6\frac{3}{4}'' \times 3\frac{1}{2}''$

# NOTICE

## SUR LA VIE ET LES OUVRAGES DE RACINE.

JEAN RACINE naquit à la Ferté - Milon le 21 décembre 1639 : il apprit le latin au college de Beauvais, et le grec sous Claude Lancelot, sacristain de Port-Royal. Ce savant homme, auteur de plusieurs ouvrages utiles, le mit, dit-on, en moins d'un an, en état d'entendre Euripide et Sophocle. L'expérience prouve qu'il n'y a aucune langue, ni même aucune science, dans laquelle, avec de l'application, de l'aptitude, et, ce qui est plus rare encore, de bons maîtres, on ne puisse faire des progrès assez rapides : mais la langue grecque est si étendue, si abondante; ses formes sont si variées, si hardies; et la plupart des mots qui la composent ont des nuances si délicates, si fugitives, et cependant si distinctes pour qui sait les saisir, qu'on persuadera difficilement à ceux qui ont fait une étude approfondie de cette langue, que neuf ou dix mois, un an même, si l'on veut, aient suffi à Racine pour bien entendre Euripide, et sur-tout Sophocle, dont les chœurs ne sont pas sans obscurités, même pour les meilleurs critiques.

Racine montra dès ses premieres années un goût très vif pour la poésie. Son plus grand plaisir étoit d'aller s'enfoncer dans les bois, dont le vaste silence est si

Racine: *Œuvres*

Paris: F. A. Didot l'aîné, 1783

$7\frac{3}{4}'' \times 4\frac{3}{4}''$

# ESSAI

DE

# FABLES NOUVELLES

DÉDIÉES AU ROI;

SUIVIES

DE POÉSIES DIVERSES

ET D'UNE ÉPITRE

SUR LES PROGRÈS DE L'IMPRIMERIE.

PAR DIDOT FILS AÎNÉ.

A PARIS,

IMPRIMÉ PAR FRANÇ. AMBR. DIDOT L'AÎNÉ

AVEC LES CARACTERES DE FIRMIN SON 2ᵈ FILS.

M. DCC. LXXXVI.

P. Didot: *Essai de Fables nouvelles*
Paris: F. A. Didot l'aîné, 1786
$5'' \times 2\frac{3}{4}''$

## APPROBATION.

*J'ai lu par ordre de monseigneur le Garde des Sceaux un manuscrit intitulé* Essai de Fables nouvelles dédiées au Roi, suivies de Poésies diverses; *par M.* Didot *fils aîné. Ces Fables, qui, sous le titre modeste d'*Essai *, offrent une morale saine, mise en action avec beaucoup de grace et de facilité, ne peuvent que faire honneur à l'esprit et au cœur de ce jeune écrivain. A la suite des Pieces qui les accompagnent, est l'*Épître sur les progrès de l'Imprimerie, *ouvrage déja connu avantageusement, où il célebre dignement l'art que son pere exerce avec une supériorité qui fera époque dans le siecle de* Louis XVI. *Tout le recueil m'a paru digne de l'impression. A Paris, ce* 7 *octobre* 1785.

*AUBERT.*

P. Didot: *Essai de Fables nouvelles*

Paris: F. A. Didot l'aîné, 1786

$4\frac{1}{4}'' \times 2\frac{3}{8}''$

# DE IMITATIONE

# CHRISTI,

## LIBER PRIMUS.

## CAPUT PRIMUM.

*De Imitatione Christi, et contemptu omnium vanitatum mundi.*

1. QUI SEQUITUR ME, NON AMBULAT IN TENEBRIS, SED HABEBIT LUMEN VITÆ. Hæc sunt verba Christi, quibus admonemur quatenus vitam ejus et mores imitemur, si volumus veraciter illuminari, et ab omni cæcitate cordis liberari.

Summum igitur studium nostrum sit in vita Jesu Christi meditari.

2. Doctrina Christi omnes doctrinas Sanctorum præcellit : et qui spiritum ejus haberet, manna ibi absconditum inveniret.

A

Kempis: *De Imitatione Christi*

Paris: Ex typ. Fratris Regis natu proximi, 1788

$8\frac{3}{8}'' \times 5\frac{1}{8}''$

# LA CONSTITUTION

## FRANÇAISE.

---

## DÉCLARATION

### DES DROITS

### DE L'HOMME ET DU CITOYEN

Les Représentans du Peuple Français,
constitués en Assemblée Nationale,
considérant que l'ignorance, l'oubli ou le
mépris des Droits de l'Homme, sont les
seules causes des malheurs publics et de
la corruption des Gouvernemens, ont ré-
solu d'exposer, dans une Déclaration
solemnelle, les Droits naturels, inaliéna-
bles et sacrés de l'Homme, afin que cette

A

*La Constitution française*
Paris: Imprimerie Nationale, 1790
$3\frac{1}{2}'' \times 2''$

# HERMÈS,

## OU

## RECHERCHES PHILOSOPHIQUES

### SUR LA

## GRAMMAIRE UNIVERSELLE.

## LIVRE PREMIER.

### CHAPITRE I.ᵉʳ

*Introduction. Objet de tout l'Ouvrage.*

Sɪ la nature avoit destiné les hommes à vivre isolés, ils n'auroient jamais senti de penchant qui les portât à communiquer entre eux. Si elle leur avoit refusé la raison comme aux animaux d'une espèce inférieure, ils n'auroient jamais pu reconnoître les matériaux propres du discours. Or, puisque la faculté de parler est le résultat de la double énergie de nos plus nobles et de nos plus excellentes

A

J. Harris: *Hermès*

Paris: Imprimerie Nationale, 1796

$5\frac{3}{4}'' \times 3\frac{1}{4}''$

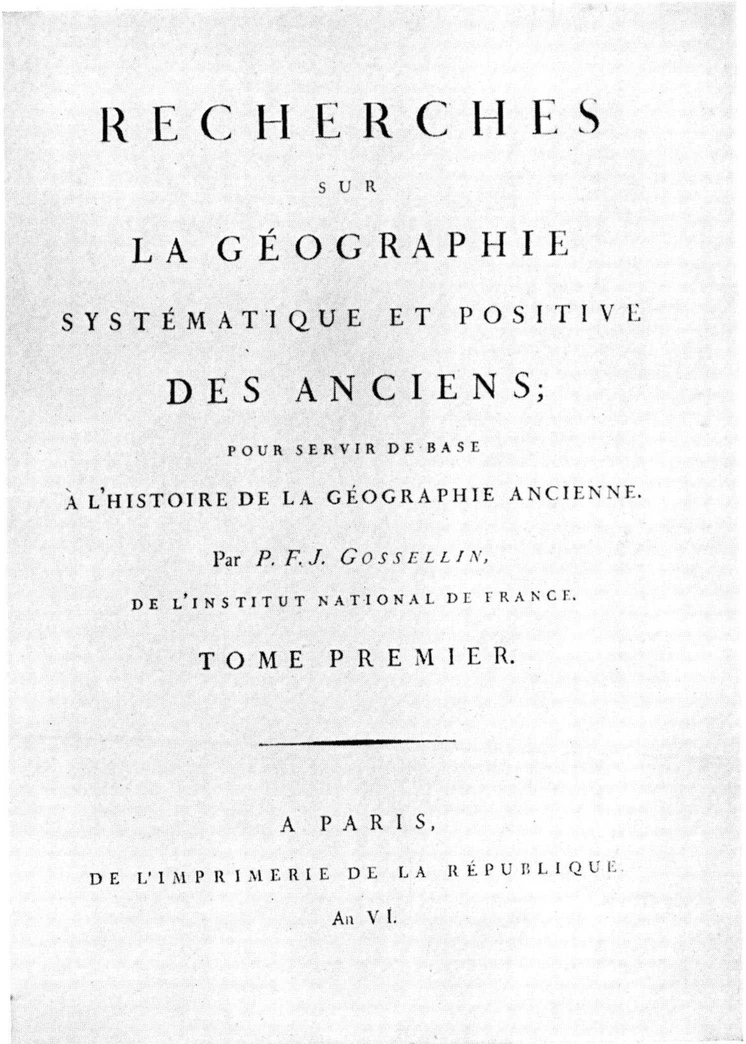

# RECHERCHES

SUR

# LA GÉOGRAPHIE

SYSTÉMATIQUE ET POSITIVE

# DES ANCIENS;

POUR SERVIR DE BASE

À L'HISTOIRE DE LA GÉOGRAPHIE ANCIENNE.

Par *P. F. J. GOSSELIN*,

DE L'INSTITUT NATIONAL DE FRANCE.

## TOME PREMIER.

———

A PARIS,

DE L'IMPRIMERIE DE LA RÉPUBLIQUE.

An VI.

Gosselin: *Recherches sur la géographie*
Paris: Imprimerie Nationale, 1798
$7\frac{5}{8}'' \times 5\frac{1}{2}''$

# LAS NAVES DE CORTES

## *DESTRUIDAS.*

### CANTO PREMIADO

## POR LA REAL ACADEMIA

## *ESPAÑOLA*

En Junta que celebró el dia 13 de Agosto de 1778.

SU AUTOR

D. JOSEPH MARÍA VACA DE GUZMAN, Doctor en ámbos Derechos, del Gremio y Claustro de la Universidad de Alcalá, y Rector actual perpetuo del Colegio de Santiago de los Caballeros Manriques de dicha Ciudad.

## MADRID.

Por D. JOACHÍN IBARRA, Impresor de Cámara de S. M.

*Con superior permiso.*

Guzman: *Las Naves de Cortes*
Madrid: Joachim Ibarra, 1778
$6\frac{7}{8}'' \times 4\frac{1}{4}''$

(1)

# ELOGIO

## DE FELIPE V.

Elogiar á un Rey, cuyo trono se vió cubierto
tantas veces del perfume de las alabanzas quando vivo, sobre cuyo sepulcro se han esparcido
despues de muerto tantas flores, y cuya grata
memoria es y será siempre plausible en los fas-
tos de la Nacion y del mundo: elogiarle á com-
petencia, como él mismo reynó, en medio del
Santuario de las Musas, y á la vista de este monu-
mento augusto, que quiso erigir su poder á la
inmortalidad de la Eloqüencia Española: elogiarle en tiempo que todavía pueden subir los
conceptos y frases del tímido Orador á los sobe-
ranos oidos del Monarca Justo, Máxîmo, Pio,
Feliz, que ciñendo la gloriosa diadema de tal
padre, es digno heredero de sus laureles y vir-
tudes: en una palabra, elogiar á FELIPE V. y
elogiarle bien, es empeño honorífico; pero tan
arduo que la dificultad se acaba de comprobar

A 2

*Elogio de Felipe V*

Madrid: Joachim Ibarra, 1779

$7\frac{1}{8}'' \times 4\frac{1}{4}''$

## PRIMERA PARTE
### DEL INGENIOSO HIDALGO
# DON QUIXOTE
## DE LA MANCHA.

### CAPÍTULO PRIMERO.

*Que trata de la condicion , y exercicio del famoso hi-*
*dalgo Don Quixote de la Mancha.*

n un Lugar de la Mancha, de cuyo nombre no quiero acordarme, no ha mucho tiempo que vivia un hidalgo de los de lanza en astillero, adarga antigua , rocin flaco, y galgo corredor. Una olla de algo mas vaca que carnero , salpicon las mas noches , duelos y quebrantos los sábados , lantejas los viernes, algun palomino de añadidura los domingos consumian las tres partes de su hacienda. El resto della concluian sayo de velarte , calzas de velludo para las fiestas con sus pantuflos de lo mesmo, y los dias de entre semana se honraba con su vello-

TOM. I.                                              A

Cervantes: *Don Quixote*

Madrid: Joachim Ibarra, 1780

$7\frac{7}{8}'' \times 5''$

# VOLTAIRE.

MAria Francisco Arouct de Voltaire, de la Academia Francesa, y de quasi todas las Sociedades literarias de Europa, nació en París en 1694, y murió en 1778.

Grandes talentos, y abuso de ellos hasta los ultimos excesos; rasgos dignos de admiracion, y una monstruosa libertad; luces capaces de honrar su siglo, y errores que son la vergüenza de él; sentimientos que ennoblecen la humanidad, y flaquezas que la degradan; la mas brillante imaginacion, el lenguaje mas cynico y repugnante; la Filosofia, y el absurdo; la erudicion, y las equivocaciones de la ignorancia; todos los encantos del entendimiento, y todas las pequeñeces de las pasiones; una rica Poesia, y manifiestos plagiarios; hermosas obras, y odiosas producciones; el atrevimiento, y la baja adulacion; las lecciones de la virtud, y la apología del vicio; los anathemas contra la envidia, y la envidia con todos sus accesos; protestas de zelo por la verdad, y todos los artificios de la mala fé; el entusiasmo de la to-

A 4                                                le-

*Decada Epistolar sobre el estado de las letras en Francia*

Madrid: Ant. de Sancha, 1781

$5\frac{3}{8}'' \times 2\frac{7}{8}''$

*Atti della solenne coronazione della insigne poetessa Maria Fernandez*

Parma: Bodoni, 1779

$5'' \times 2\frac{1}{2}''$

# THE CASTLE
## OF OTRANTO,

A

## GOTHIC STORY.

TRANSLATED

BY

# WILLIAM MARSHAL, GENT.

FROM THE ORIGINAL ITALIAN

## OF ONUPHRIO MURALTO,

CANON OF THE CHURCH OF ST. NICHOLAS

AT OTRANTO.

PARMA.

PRINTED BY BODONI, FOR

J. EDWARDS, BOOKSELLER OF LONDON.

MDCCXCI.

Muralto and Marshal: *The Castle of Otranto*

Parma: Bodoni, 1791

$5\frac{3}{4}'' \times 3''$

# THE CASTLE

OF

# OTRANTO

A

# GOTHIC STORY, &c.

---

## CHAPTER I.

*M*ANFRED, Prince of *Otranto*, had one son and one daughter: The latter a most beautiful virgin, aged eighteen, was called *Matilda*. *Conrad*, the son, was three years younger, a homely youth, sickly, and of no promising disposition; yet he was the darling of his father, who never showed any symptoms of affection to *Matilda*. *Manfred* had contracted a marriage for his son with the Marquis of *Vicenza*'s daughter,

*a*

Muralto and Marshal: *The Castle of Otranto*
Parma: Bodoni, 1791
$5\frac{7}{8}'' \times 3''$

DEGLI

# ANNALI

DI

## C. CORNELIO TACITO

### LIBRO PRIMO.

Sesto Pompejo, e Sesto Apulejo Consoli,
Nerone Claudio Druso Cesare,
e Cajo Norbano Consoli.

I.

Roma nascente fu dominata da' Regi. Stettero per fatto di Bruto la libertà, e il Consolato. Le Dittature eran temporanee, nè il potere Decemvirale prevalse più d'un biennio, nè lungamente l'autorità Consolare de' militari Tribuni. Non Cinna, non Sulla ritennero durevolmente il dominio, e in breve si concentrarono la possanza di Pompejo e di Crasso in Cesare, e l'armi di Lepido e d'Antonio in Augusto, che la Repubblica, stancata dalle civili discordie, occupò col titolo di

Tacitus: *Opera*

Parma: Bodoni, 1795

$7\frac{5}{8}'' \times 4\frac{1}{2}''$

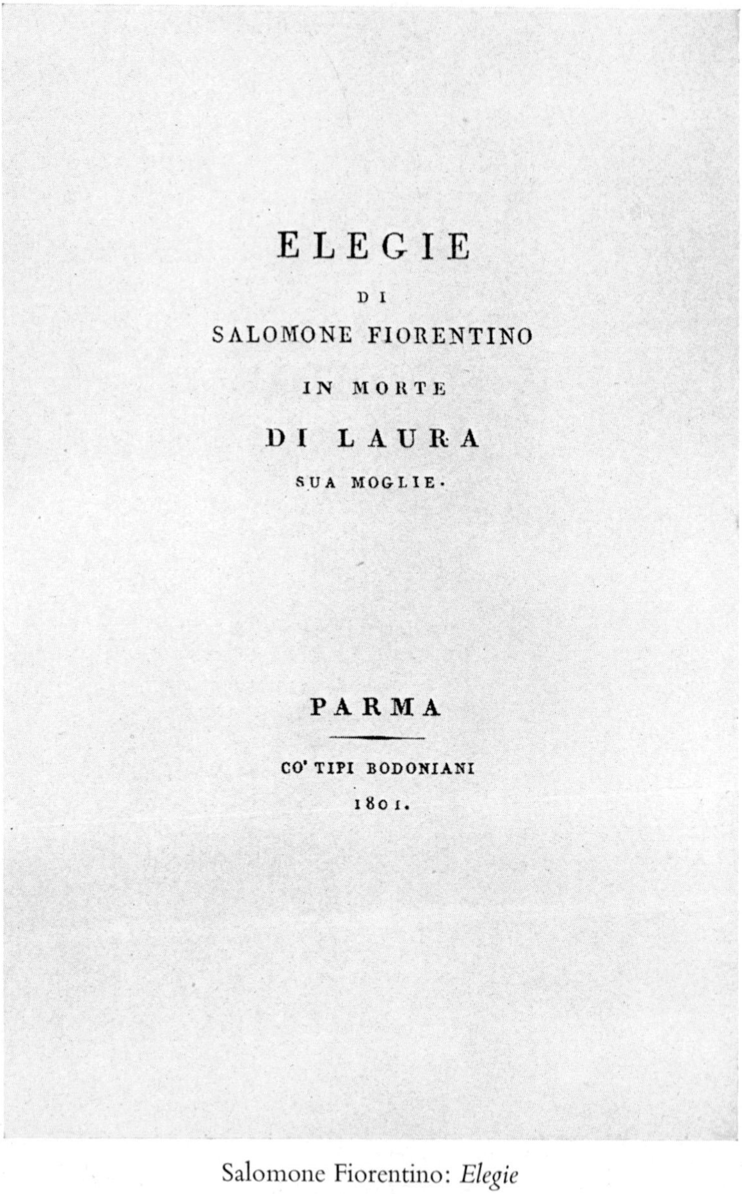

# ELEGIE

D I

SALOMONE FIORENTINO

IN MORTE

## DI LAURA

SUA MOGLIE.

## PARMA

CO' TIPI BODONIANI

1801.

Salomone Fiorentino: *Elegie*

Parma: Bodoni, 1801

$3'' \times 1\frac{3}{4}''$

# PIETAS
# Universitatis Oxonienfis
### In *OBITUM* Auguftiffimi Regis
# GULIELMI III.
### ET
## *GRATULATIO*
### In exoptatiffimam Sereniffimæ
# ANNÆ REGINÆ
## *INAUGURATIONEM.*

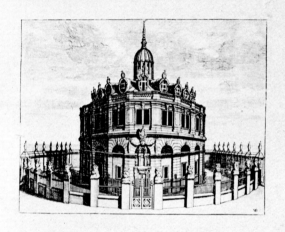

## *OXONII,* E THEATRO SHELDONIANO,
### *An. Dom.* MDCCII.

*Pietas Univ. Oxon. in obitum Gulielmi III.*

Oxford University Press, 1702

$10\frac{1}{4}'' \times 5\frac{1}{2}''$

# *ANNE* R.

ANNE, by the Grace of God, Queen of *England*, *Scotland*, *France*, and *Ireland*, Defender of the Faith, *&c.* To all to whom These Presents shall come Greeting. Whereas Our Trusty and Wellbeloved *William Delaune*, Doctor in Divinity, and Vice-Chancellor of Our University of *Oxford*, has humbly represented unto Us, in the behalf of the said University, that They have at a Great Expence already Published One Volume of the late Earl of *Clarendon*'s History, and intend in a short time to Publish the Second and Third Volumes for Compleating the Work ; and the sole Right of the Copy of the said Work being Vested in Our University of *Oxford*, and They having humbly besought Us to Grant Them Our Royal Priviledge and Licence for the sole Printing and Publishing the same for the Term of Fourteen Years; We being Graciously enclined to encourage the said Undertaking, are pleased to condescend to their Request; and do therefore hereby Give and Grant unto Our said University of *Oxford*, Our Royal Licence and Priviledge, for the sole Printing and Publishing the said Three Volumes of the late Earl of *Clarendon*'s History, for and during the Term of Fourteen Years, to be computed from the Day of the Date hereof; strictly Charging, Prohibiting, and Forbidding all Our Subjects to Reprint or Abridge the said History, or any Part of it, or to Import, Buy, Vend, Utter, or Distribute any Copies of the same, or any Part thereof, Reprinted beyond the Seas, within the said Term, without the Consent and Approbation of Our said University first had and Obtained, as They and every of them Offending herein will Answer the Contrary at their Peril, and such other Penalties as by the Laws and Statutes of this Our Realm may be inflicted ; Whereof the Master, Wardens, and Company of Stationers of Our City of *London*, the Commissioners and Officers of our Customs, and all other Our Officers and Ministers whom it may concern, are to take Notice, that due Obedience be given to Our Pleasure herein signified. Given at Our Court at *Hampton*-Court the 24th day of *June* 1703. In the Second Year of Our Reign.

By Her Majesties Command.

C. *Hedges.*

Clarendon: *History of the Rebellion*

Oxford University Press, 1704

$12'' \times 6\frac{1}{4}''$

# M. Tullii Ciceronis
# TUSCULANARUM
## DISPUTATIONUM
### *L I B R I* V.

Ex recenſione

# *JOANNIS DAVISII,*
#### Coll. Regin. Cantab. Socii.

### Cum Ejuſdem COMMENTARIO.

## *CANTABRIGIÆ,*

##### Typis Academicis.

Impenſis *EDM. JEFFERY*, Bibliopolæ Cantabr.

Proſtant venales *LONDINI* apud Jac. Knapton,
in Cœmeterio D. Pauli. MDCCVIII.

Cicero: *Tusculanae Disputationes*

Cambridge University Press, 1708

$6\frac{1}{8}'' \times 3\frac{1}{2}''$

THE

# WORKS

OF

Mr. *ALEXANDER POPE.*

CICERO pro ARCH.

*Hæc ftudia adolefcentiam alunt, feneƈutem obleƈant; fecundas res ornant, adverfis perfugium & folatium præbent; deleƈant domi, non impedunt foris; pernoƈant nobifcum, peregrinantur, rufticantur.*

*LONDON:*

Printed by W. BOWYER, for BERNARD LINTOT between the *Temple-Gates.* 1717.

Alexander Pope: *Works*

London: W. Bowyer, 1717

$9\frac{7}{8}'' \times 5\frac{5}{8}''$

# PUBLII VIRGILII

## MARONIS

# BUCOLICA,

# GEORGICA,

*E T*

# AENEIS.

*B I R M I N G H A M I AE:*

Typis JOHANNIS BASKERVILLE.

MDCCLVII.

Virgil: *Bucolica, etc.*

Birmingham: Baskerville, 1757

$8\frac{1}{2}'' \times 5\frac{1}{2}''$

## P. VIRGILII MARONIS

# BUCOLICA

*ECLOGA* I. cui nomen *TITYRUS.*

MELIBOEUS, TITYRUS.

TITYRE, tu patulæ recubans sub tegmine fagi
Silvestrem tenui Musam meditaris avena:
Nos patriæ fines, et dulcia linquimus arva;
Nos patriam fugimus: tu, Tityre, lentus in umbra
5 Formosam resonare doces Amaryllida silvas.
    *T.* O Melibœe, Deus nobis hæc otia fecit:
Namque erit ille mihi semper Deus: illius aram
Sæpe tener nostris ab ovilibus imbuet agnus.
Ille meas errare boves, ut cernis, et ipsum
10 Ludere, quæ vellem, calamo permisit agresti.
    *M.* Non equidem invideo; miror magis: undique totis
Usque adeo turbatur agris. en ipse capellas
Protenus æger ago: hanc etiam vix, Tityre, duco:
Hic inter densas corylos modo namque gemellos,
15 Spem gregis, ah! filice in nuda connixa reliquit.
Sæpe malum hoc nobis, si mens non læva fuisset,
De cœlo tactas memini prædicere quercus:
Sæpe sinistra cava prædixit ab ilice cornix.
Sed tamen, iste Deus qui sit, da, Tityre, nobis.
20     *T.* Urbem, quam dicunt Romam, Melibœe, putavi
Stultus ego huic nostræ similem, quo sæpe solemus
Pastores ovium teneros depellere fœtus.
Sic canibus catulos similes, sic matribus hœdos

           A                   Noram;

Virgil: *Bucolica, etc.*

Birmingham: Baskerville, 1757

$8\frac{1}{2}'' \times 5\frac{1}{4}''$

# ORLANDO

## FURIOSO

### DI

## LODOVICO

# ARIOSTO.

*TOMO PRIMO.*

*BIRMINGHAM,*

Da' Torchj di G. BASKERVILLE:

Per P. MOLINI Librajo dell' Accademia
Reale, e G. MOLINI.

**M. DCC. LXXIII.**

Ariosto: *Orlando Furioso*
Birmingham: Baskerville, 1773
$6\frac{1}{2}'' \times 3\frac{3}{4}''$

# FUGITIVE PIECES
### I N
## VERSE and PROSE.

*Pereunt et imputantur.*

## PRINTED AT STRAWBERRY-HILL.
### M DCC LVIII.

Walpole: *Fugitive Pieces*

Strawberry Hill, 1758

$5\frac{1}{8}'' \times 3''$

# FUGITIVE PIECES.

# V E R S E S

## IN MEMORY OF

## KING HENRY the SIXTH,

Founder of KING's-COLLEGE, CAMBRIDGE.

*[Written February 2, 1738.]*

WHILE Superstition teaches to revere
    The sainted Calendar and letter'd
        year;
While Bigots joy in canonizing Shades,
Fictitious Martyrs, visionary Maids;
Haste, Gratitude, and hail this better day;
At HENRY's shrine present thy votive lay;
If this peculiarly for His be known,
Whose Charity made ev'ry day his own.

            B                But

Walpole: *Fugitive Pieces*

Strawberry Hill, 1758

$4\frac{3}{4}'' \times 2\frac{7}{8}''$

# C. PLINII CÆCILII

## SECUNDI

# EPISTOLARUM

## LIBRI X.

SUMPTIBUS EDITORIS EXCUDEBANT

M. RITCHIE & J. SAMMELLS

L O N D I N I

M. DCC. XC.

Pliny: *Epistolae*

London: Typis Edmundi Fry, 1790

$3\frac{3}{4}'' \times 2\frac{5}{8}''$

# C. PLINII CÆCILII

## SECUNDI

# EPISTOLARUM

## LIBER SEPTIMUS.

### I. C. PLINIUS SECUNDUS RESTITUTO
### SUO S.

TERRET me hæc tua tam pertinax valetudo, & quanquam te temperatiſſimum noverim, vereor tamen, ne quid illi etiam in mores tuos liceat. Proinde moneo, patienter reſiſtas. Hoc laudabile, hoc ſalutare admittit humana natura. Quod ſuadeo, ipſe certe ſic agere ſanus cum meis ſoleo. Spero quidem, ſi forte in adverſam valetudinem incidero, nihil me deſideraturum vel pudore, vel pœniténtia dignum : Si tamen ſuperaverit morbus, denuncio, ne quid mihi detur, niſi permittentibus medicis, ſciantque, ſi dederint, ita vindicaturum, ut ſolent alii, quæ negantur. Quinetiam cum peruſtus ardentiſſima febri, tandem remiſſus, unctuſque acciperem à medico potionem, porrexi manum, ut-

Pliny: *Epistolae*

London: Typis Edmundi Fry, 1790

$4\frac{3}{8}'' \times 2\frac{5}{8}''$

R

# THE

# FLORIST'S DIRECTORY.

## On HYACINTHS.

**D**OUBLE Hyacinths, which are
much more beautiful and eſtima-
ble than thoſe which produce ſingle flowers, are, like the latter, known by the
general diſtinction of Reds, Whites, and
Blues, with a few kinds of Yellow,
more recently obtained from ſeed.   In
many inſtances, Double Hyacinths have
the

Maddock: *The Florist's Directory*

London: S. Couchman, 1792

$5\frac{7}{8}'' \times 3\frac{1}{8}''$

# THE

# ŒCONOMY

OF

# HUMAN LIFE.

TRANSLATED FROM

## AN INDIAN MANUSCRIPT,

## WRITTEN BY AN ANCIENT BRAMIN.

TO WHICH IS PREFIXED

AN ACCOUNT OF THE MANNER IN WHICH THE SAID
MANUSCRIPT WAS DISCOVERED.

IN A

# LETTER

## FROM AN ENGLISH GENTLEMAN NOW RESIDING IN CHINA

*TO THE EARL OF E\*\*\*\*.*

London:

PRINTED BY T. RICKABY,

FOR I. AND E. HARDING, PALL-MALL.

1795.

*Œconomy of Human Life*

London: T. Rickaby, 1795

$4\frac{7}{8}'' \times 2\frac{7}{8}''$

POEMS

BY

GOLDSMITH

AND

PARNELL.

LONDON:

PRINTED BY W. BULMER AND CO.

Shakspeare Printing Office,

CLEVELAND-ROW.

1795.

Goldsmith and Parnell: *Poems*

London: W. Bulmer, 1795

$6\frac{7}{8}'' \times 3\frac{7}{8}''$

## ADVERTISEMENT

To raise the Art of Printing in this country
from the neglected state in which it had long
been suffered to continue, and to remove the
opprobrium which had but too justly been attached to the late productions of the English
press, much has been done within the last few
years; and the warm emulation which has discovered itself amongst the Printers of the present
day, as well in the remote parts of the kingdom
as in the metropolis, has been highly patronized
by the public in general. The present volume,
in addition to the SHAKSPEARE, the MILTON,
and many other valuable works of elegance,
which have already been given to the world,
through the medium of the Shakspeare Press,
are particularly meant to combine the various

Goldsmith and Parnell: *Poems*
London: W. Bulmer, 1795
$7'' \times 4\frac{7}{8}''$

The chase I sing, hounds, and their various breed,
And no less various use.  O thou, great Prince!
Whom Cambria's towering hills proclaim their lord,
Deign thou to hear my bold, instructive song.
While grateful citizens, with pompous show,
Rear the triumphal arch, rich with the exploits
Of thy illustrious house; while virgins pave
Thy way with flowers, and as the royal youth
Passing they view, admire, and sigh in vain;
While crowded theatres, too fondly proud
Of their exotick minstrels, and shrill pipes,
The price of manhood, hail thee with a song.

Somerville: *The Chase*
London: W. Bulmer, 1796
$6\frac{3}{4}'' \times 4\frac{5}{8}''$

# THE
# SEASONS,

BY

# James Thomson.

ILLUSTRATED WITH

# ENGRAVINGS

BY

*F. BARTOLOZZI, R. A.* AND *P. W. TOMKINS,*

Hiſtorical Engravers to Their Majeſties;

FROM

# ORIGINAL PICTURES

PAINTED FOR THE WORK

BY

*W. HAMILTON, R. A.*

---

LONDON:

PRINTED FOR P. W. TOMKINS, NEW BOND-STREET.

*THE LETTER-PRESS BY T. BENSLEY.*

*THE TYPES BY V. FIGGINS.*

MDCCXCVII

Thomson: *The Seasons*

London: T. Bensley, 1797

$13\frac{3}{8}'' \times 8\frac{5}{8}''$

# REMARKS

ON

# CAVALRY;

BY THE PRUSSIAN MAJOR GENERAL OF HUSSARS,

## *WARNERY.*

TRANSLATED FROM THE ORIGINAL.

### London :

*PRINTED FOR THE TRANSLATOR,*

AND SOLD BY

T. EDGERTON, MILITARY LIBRARY, WHITEHALL;
AND T. GARDINER, No. 19, PRINCES-STREET, CAVENDISH-SQUARE.
AND MAY BE HAD OF THE BOOKSELLERS.

PRINTED BY J. BARFIELD, No. 91, WARDOUR-STREET, SOHO.

1798.

C. E. de Warnery: *Remarks on Cavalry*

London: J. Barfield, 1798

$8\frac{3}{8}'' \times 5\frac{1}{4}''$

*ADDRESS TO THE WORLD,*

BY

MR. BELL,

*British-Library, Strand, London.*

I HAVE perceived with regret that the ART OF PRINTING has been very much neglected IN ENGLAND, and that it is still in a declining state---expedition being attended to rather than excellence---and temporary gain is preferred to lasting advantage and reputation ;----notwithstanding ENGLAND's inattention to *this art*, which is considered as the happiest invention that ever employed the faculties of man---it is worthy of notice, that FRANCE, SPAIN, ITALY, and GERMANY, are contending for the honours of the *Press*, under the sanction and encouragement of their respective SOVEREIGNS.

To retrieve and exalt the *neglected* ART OF PRINTING in ENGLAND is the present

John Bell: *Prospectus*

London: Bell, 1788

$5\frac{5}{8}'' \times 3\frac{5}{8}''$

# SPECIMEN

OF

## *BELL's*

# NEW PRINTING TYPES,

*Which have been completed under his Directions,*

### AT THE BRITISH LETTER FOUNDRY,

By WILLIAM COLMAN, *Regulator,*
And RICHARD AUSTIN, *Punch-Cutter.*

### *PRINTERS IN GENERAL*

May be now furnished with these original *Types*, at
the Prices usually charged for common Types, by
applying to the *Founder,*

*J. BELL,* British-Library, *Strand, London.*

139

Bell: *Specimen*

London: Bell, 1788

$6\frac{1}{8}'' \times 3\frac{1}{2}''$

# BELL's

## *CLASSICAL ARRANGEMENT*

### OF

# FUGITIVE POETRY.

#### VOL. V.

Though redolent of ev'ry flow'r
That once perfum'd Hymettus' side,
No hoarded sweets of Grecian store
Did e'er the Attic bee provide,
That could a purer flavor yield,
Than yields the comb this hive contains,
Though cull'd from no Hesperian field,
But the wild growth of Britain's plains.

### *LONDON:*

PRINTED BY
JOHN BELL, British Library, STRAND,
Bookseller to His Royal Highness the PRINCE of WALES.
M DCC LXXXIX.

*Fugitive Poetry*
London: Bell, 1789
$4\frac{7}{8}'' \times 2\frac{3}{4}''$

# MÉMORIAL

## TOPOGRAPHIQUE ET MILITAIRE,

REDIGE

AU DÉPÔT GÉNÉRAL DE LA GUERRE;

IMPRIMÉ PAR ORDRE DU MINISTRE.

---

N.º 1. TOPOGRAPHIE.

---

III.ᵉ Trimestre de l'an X.

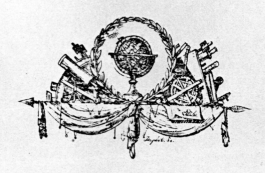

A PARIS,

DE L'IMPRIMERIE DE LA RÉPUBLIQUE.

Vendémiaire an XI.

---

*Mémorial topographique et militaire*

Paris: Imprimerie Nationale, 1803

$6\frac{1}{8}'' \times 4''$

# MÉMORIAL
# TOPOGRAPHIQUE
## ET MILITAIRE.

## *SECTION PREMIÈRE.*

### CHAPITRE I.er
#### GÉOGRAPHIE.

*NOTICE historique et analytique sur la Construction des Cartes géographiques.*

#### S. I.er
##### HISTORIQUE.

DANS l'origine, la géographie ne consistait qu'en des descriptions plus ou moins bien faites. On cherchait à peindre, pour ainsi dire, par écrit, les lieux dont on parlait ; on les désignait par les qualités qui leur convenaient le plus ; et les poésies d'Homère nous en fournissent plus d'une preuve : toutes les villes dont ce poëte a

# ALPHABET IRLANDAIS,

## PRÉCÉDÉ

## D'UNE NOTICE HISTORIQUE,

## LITTÉRAIRE ET TYPOGRAPHIQUE,

PAR J. J. MARCEL,

DIRECTEUR DE L'IMPRIMERIE DE LA RÉPUBLIQUE.

## A PARIS,

DE L'IMPRIMERIE DE LA RÉPUBLIQUE.

NIVOSE AN XII.

Marcel: *Alphabet irlandais*
Paris: Imprimerie Nationale, 1804
$6\frac{3}{8}'' \times 3\frac{3}{4}''$

# RECHERCHES

SUR

## LA DÉCOUVERTE

## DE L'ESSENCE DE ROSE,

PAR L. LANGLÈS,

MEMBRE DE L'INSTITUT NATIONAL,
CONSERVATEUR DES MANUSCRITS
ORIENTAUX, &c.

---

جو بلبلان نزول كنم اشيان كل

Comme les rossignols, nous reposons sur les roses.

HHÂFIZ.

---

A PARIS,

DE L'IMPRIMERIE IMPÉRIALE.

AN XIII = 1804 [v. s.].

---

Langlès: *Recherches sur la découverte de l'essence de Rose*

Paris: ImprimerieImpériale, 1804

$3\frac{1}{2}'' \times 2''$

# PRÉCIS

## DES GUERRES

### DES RUSSES

### CONTRE LES TURCS.

## CHAPITRE PREMIER.

### LES TURCS AU DIX-SEPTIEME SIÈCLE.

Montecuculli, aussi bon écrivain militaire que grand capitaine, nous présente les Turcs comme des modèles à imiter à la guerre, tant pour la sagesse avec laquelle ils l'entreprennent que pour leur manière de la conduire. Leurs marches, leurs campements, leurs dispositions pour le combat, lui paraissent également dignes d'éloges;

Langlès: *Précis des Guerres des Russes*

Paris: Firmin Didot, 1828

$5\frac{5}{8}'' \times 3\frac{3}{4}''$

# INSCRIPTIONS
# ANTIQVES
## DE LYON

REPRODVITES D'APRES LES MONVMENTS OV RECVEILLIES DANS LES AVTEVRS

PAR

## ALPH DE BOISSIEV

LOVIS PERRIN IMPRIMEVR A LYON

MDCCCXLVI — MDCCCLIV

Boissieu: *Inscriptions antiques*

Lyons: Perrin, 1846

$9\frac{1}{2}'' \times 6\frac{3}{4}''$

S

TROUVAILLE DE SMYRNE

ANS le courant de 1880, une heureuse circonftance me permit d'acquérir une trouvaille entière de deniers de billon romains, faite, quelque temps aupa- ravant, dans les environs de Smyrne. Cette trouvaille fe compofait de 586 pièces, dont je donne le détail ci-deffous, & comprenait, dans fon enfemble, 23 perfonnages : empereurs, impératrices, céfars & tyrans, commençant à l'em- pereur Philippe père pour finir au règne de Carus, embraf- fant donc la période qui fépare Gordien III de Dioclétien, époque la plus trifte, en même temps que la plus obfcure de l'hiftoire de l'empire romain.

Ces temps, cependant fi mouvementés, où l'hiftoire ne nous tranfmet, pour ainfi dire, que des récits de crimes, font encore

Boissieu: *Trouvaille de Smyrne*

Lyons: Perrin, 1880

$7\frac{5}{8}'' \times 4\frac{7}{8}''$

# NOTICE SUR LA VIE

## ET LES ŒUVRES DE BERTIN

 ERS *la fin du* XVIII<sup>e</sup> *siècle, alors que Dorat et son école brillaient de tout leur faux éclat, et qu'André Chénier n'avait encore écrit, même pour ses amis, aucun de ces vers qui devaient renouveler la poésie vieillissante, la France vit apparaître un jeune poète qui, né sous un ciel plus chaud, élevé dans l'étude, non des Grecs, il est vrai, comme l'auteur de* l'Aveugle, *mais des Latins, dont il s'était pénétré, vint heureusement remplacer le cliquetis de mots et d'idées, alors si fort à la mode, par une vivacité, une tendresse d'expressions, nées de sentiments vrais, et dont il avait déjà trouvé les modèles dans l'an-*

a

Bertin: *Poésies*

Paris: Quantin, 1879

$4\frac{7}{8}'' \times 2\frac{3}{4}''$

# LES AMOURS

## LIVRE·PREMIER

### ÉLÉGIE I

JE chantois les combats : étranger au Parnasse,
Peut-être ma jeunesse excusoit mon audace :
Sur deux lignes rangés, mes vers présomptueux
Déployoient, en deux temps, six pieds majestueux.
　　　De ces vers nombreux et sublimes
　　　L'Amour se riant à l'écart,
　　Sur mon papier mit la main au hasard,
Retrancha quelques pieds, brouilla toutes les rimes
De ce désordre heureux naquit un nouvel art.

Bertin: *Poésies*

Paris: Quantin, 1879

$5\frac{1}{8}'' \times 2\frac{5}{8}''$

# DE LA MOTHE-FÉNELON

# FABLES

COMPOSÉES POUR

## L'ÉDUCATION DU DUC DE BOURGOGNE

AVEC UNE PRÉFACE

PAR

## HIPPOLYTE FOURNIER

PARIS

**LIBRAIRIE DES BIBLIOPHILES**

Rue Saint-Honoré, 338

M DCCC LXXXIV

Fénelon: *Fables*

Paris: Jouaust, 1884

$4\frac{3}{8}'' \times 2\frac{5}{8}''$

# FABLES

## COMPOSÉES POUR L'ÉDUCATION

DE FEU MONSEIGNEUR

## LE DUC DE BOURGOGNE

### FABLE I

#### LES AVANTURES D'ARISTONOUS

OPHRONIME, ayant perdu les biens de ses ancêtres par des naufrages et par d'autres malheurs, s'en consoloit par sa vertu dans l'isle de Delos. Là il chantoit sur une lyre d'or les merveilles du Dieu qu'on y adore. Il cultivoit les Muses, dont il étoit aimé; il recherchoit curieusement tous les secrets de la nature, le cours des astres et des cieux,

Fénelon: *Fables*

Paris: Jouaust, 1884

$4\frac{7}{8}'' \times 2\frac{5}{8}''$

CINQUIÈME PARTIE

LA GRAVURE INTRODUITE DANS LE LIVRE

JEAN DU PRÉ

VEC l'imprimeur Jean Du Pré commence une nouvelle ère pour la typographie française. Jean Du Pré est le premier typographe parisien qui ait introduit la gravure dans les livres. Le 22 septembre 1481, il publie un Missel de l'Église de Paris, dans lequel on remarque deux grandes gravures sur bois : le Père éternel & le Christ en croix, placées au Canon de la Messe. Le 28 novembre suivant, il termine un Missel de Verdun, qui contient des gravures sur bois & sur métal, en relief, imitant les ornements des manuscrits.

Christian: *Origines de l'Imprimerie française*

Paris: Imprimerie Nationale, 1900

$8\frac{1}{2}'' \times 5\frac{3}{4}''$

# A LA MÉMOIRE

## DE

# JEAN GUTENBERG

## HOMMAGE

### DE L'IMPRIMERIE NATIONALE

#### ET

### DE LA BIBLIOTHÈQUE NATIONALE

### PARIS

#### IMPRIMERIE NATIONALE

#### JUIN MDCCCC

*Hommage à Jean Gutenberg*
Paris: Imprimerie Nationale, 1900
$13\frac{3}{4}'' \times 9\frac{1}{4}''$

ANATOLE FRANCE
DE L'ACADÉMIE FRANÇAISE

# LA RÔTISSERIE
## DE LA
# REINE PÉDAUQUE

ILLUSTRÉE PAR AUGUSTE LEROUX
DE 176 COMPOSITIONS
GRAVÉES PAR
DUPLESSIS, ERNEST FLORIAN, LES DEUX FROMENT
GUSMAN ET PERRICHON

ÉDITIONS D'ART
ÉDOUARD PELLETAN
125, BOULEVARD SAINT-GERMAIN, 125
PARIS

1911

France: *La Rôtisserie de la reine Pédauque*

Paris: Édouard Pelletan, 1907

$7'' \times 5''$

## I

### LES RAISONS
### D'UNE RÉSURRECTION.

L'ITALIE contemporaine va célébrer, en compagnie des nations invitées, le cinquantième anniversaire de ce qu'elle-même a appelé sa *Résurrection,* son *Risorgimento,* comme État parmi les États, comme peuple au milieu des peuples. A cette sorte d'exposition éternelle de la beauté que lui font les paysages de sa nature et les chefs-d'œuvre de son passé, l'Italie entend ajouter deux grandes Expositions universelles, l'une à Turin, d'où s'arma le *Risorgimento,* l'autre à Rome, où il se couronna.

Turin recevra du monde entier l'industrie et les sciences, Rome en accueillera les arts et l'histoire. Qu'il s'agisse de l'automobile ou de l'avia-

III.                                                    19

Bérenger: *Les Résurrections italiennes*

Paris: Édouard Pelletan, 1911

$6\frac{1}{2}'' \times 4\frac{3}{8}''$

une heure. Les sentiments qui nous la rendent ou douce, ou du moins tolérable, naissent d'un mensonge et se nourrissent d'illusions.

Si, possédant, comme Dieu, la vérité, l'unique vérité, un homme la laissait tomber de ses mains, le monde en serait anéanti sur le coup et l'univers se dissiperait aussitôt comme une ombre. La vérité divine, ainsi qu'un jugement dernier, le réduirait en poudre.

Nous avons mangé les fruits de l'arbre de la science, et il nous est resté dans la bouche un goût de cendre. Nous avons exploré la terre; nous nous sommes mêlés aux races noires, rouges et jaunes, et nous

148

Hesiod: *Les Travaux*

Paris: Édouard Pelletan, 1912

$7\frac{3}{4}'' \times 4\frac{3}{4}''$

# ANNALES

### DE LA

## CITÉ DE GENÈVE.

\* \*

G ENEVE defia ville iadis puiffante & floriffante, plus grande 3. fois en fes feuls fauxbourgs qu'elle n'eft a prefent, en cefte affiette remarquable fur cefte petite mer du tant renomme lac Leman & fur l'eftendue de la meilleure part du pays voifin iufques a la ville de Solleure, a tou-fiours demeuré ville franche & Republique imperialle voire plufieurs fiecles auant que la maifon de Sauoye euft encor aucun nom ni commencement, releuant fimplement & immediatement de l'Empire Romain fans qu'il y ait memoire ni acte vallable du contraire, gouuernee par fes confuls ou fyndiques & autres ma-giftrats, regie par fes propres loix, ftatuts & edicts municipaux & hors iceux par le droit efcript imperial duquel mefmes iceux edicts font pour la plufpart extraicts & tirez , n'ayant a prince ou potentat du monde aucun debuoir ni obligation de fubiection &

a . i.

*Annales de la cité de Genève*

Geneva: Fick, 1858

$6\frac{1}{4}'' \times 3\frac{3}{8}''$

## NOTES ET DOCUMENTS.

\* \*
\*

### TABLEAV GENEALOGIQVE DES PRINCES
de la maifon de Savoie jufqu'à la bienheureufe
Louife, pour fervir à fon hiftoire.

'ORIGINE *de la maifon de Savoie,
qui règne depuis huit fiècles, eft à
peine connue. Ses princes font per-
fuadés qu'ils defcendent de Bérold de
Saxe, iffu lui-même de la famille du
grand Vittikind, contemporain de
Charlemagne. Un roi de Bourgogne,
nommé Rodolphe, donna à Bérold à perpétuité, pour lui &
fes defcendants, en récompenfe de fes fervices, le comté de
Maurienne & les feigneuries qui l'environnent. Cette cef-
fion eft datée d'Aix, du 5 des ides de Mai de l'an 1000.*

*Les favantes recherches de M. le commandeur Cibrario
fur l'origine de la maifon de Savoie ont fait rejeter cette
opinion. L'illuftre écrivain a prouvé que cette puiffante dy-
naftie eft originaire d'Italie.*

*Nous avons cru devoir donner ici un tableau chronolo-
gique des princes qui ont illuftré cette grande famille, la
plus ancienne de toutes les maifons royales aujourd'hui ré-
gnantes.*

*I. — BEROLD DE SAXE, fuivant Pingon, Guiche-
non, &c., vivait l'an 1020. Il fe maria avec Catherine de
Bavière dont il eut un fils nommé Humbert.*

*Vie de très illustre dame Madame Loyse de Savoye*

Geneva: Fick, 1860

$6\frac{3}{8}'' \times 3\frac{3}{8}''$

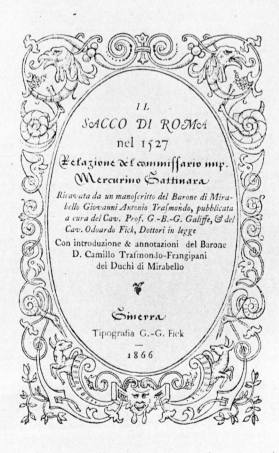

Gattinara: *Il sacco di Roma*

Geneva: Fick, 1866

$4'' \times 2\frac{5}{8}''$

# CHRONIQVES
## DE GENEVE
*par FRANCOIS BONIVARD*
prieur de Saint-Victor

PVBLIEES PAR
GVSTAVE REVILLIOD

\*

Tome Premier

GENEVE
*Imprimerie de Jules-G. Fick*
rue du Puits Saint-Pierre, 4

\*

1867

Bonivard: *Chroniques de Genève*

Geneva: Fick, 1867

$5\frac{5}{8}'' \times 3\frac{1}{4}''$

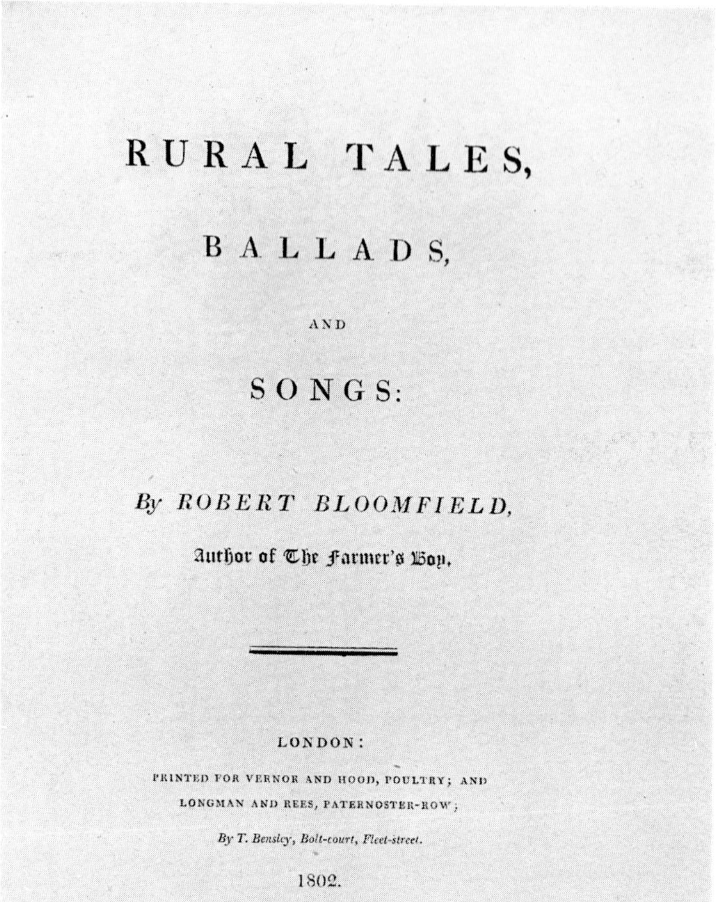

# RURAL TALES,

## BALLADS,

AND

## SONGS:

*By ROBERT BLOOMFIELD,*

Author of The Farmer's Boy,

———————

LONDON:

PRINTED FOR VERNOR AND HOOD, POULTRY; AND
LONGMAN AND REES, PATERNOSTER-ROW;

*By T. Bensley, Bolt-court, Fleet-street.*

1802.

Bloomfield: *Rural Tales, Ballads, and Songs*
London: T. Bensley, 1802
$5\frac{7}{8}'' \times 3\frac{3}{8}''$

A N

## INTRODUCTORY LETTER

TO THE

### *Right Honourable Earl COWPER.*

---

*YOUR family, my Lord, our country itself, and the whole literary world, sustained such a loss in the death of that amiable Man, and enchanting Author, who forms the subject of these Volumes, as inspired the friends of genius and virtue with universal concern. It soon became a general wish, that some authentic, and copious memorial of a character so highly interesting should be produced with all becoming dispatch; not only to render due honour to the dead, but to alleviate the regret of a nation taking a just, and liberal pride in the reputation of a Poet, who had obtained, and deserved, her applause, her esteem, her affection. If this laudable wish was very sensibly felt by the public at large, it glowed with peculiar warmth and eagerness in the bosom of the few, who had been so fortunate as to enjoy an intimacy with Cowper in some unclouded periods of his life, and who knew from such an intimacy, that a lively sweetness,*

a                                        *and*

Hayley: *Life of William Cowper*

Chichester: J. Seagrave, 1803

$6\frac{3}{4}'' \times 5\frac{3}{8}''$

I

THE

# LAY

OF

# THE LAST MINSTREL,

A POEM;

BY

## WALTER SCOTT, Esq.

*Dum relego, scripsisse pudet, quia plurima cerno,*
*Me quoque, qui feci, judice, digna lini.*

**LONDON:**
PRINTED FOR LONGMAN, HURST, REES, AND ORME,
PATERNOSTER-ROW, AND A. CONSTABLE AND CO. EDINBURGH;
*By James Ballantyne & Co. Edinburgh.*
1806.

Scott: *Lay of the Last Minstrel*
Edinburgh: Ballantyne, 1806
$5\frac{3}{8}'' \times 2\frac{7}{8}''$

# INTRODUCTION.

———

THE way was long, the wind was cold,
The Minstrel was infirm and old;
His withered cheek, and tresses gray,
Seemed to have known a better day;
The harp, his sole remaining joy,
Was carried by an orphan boy.
The last of all the bards was he,
Who sung of Border chivalry;
For, well-a-day! their date was fled,
His tuneful brethren all were dead;
And he, neglected and oppressed,
Wished to be with them, and at rest.
No more, on prancing palfrey borne,
He carolled, light as lark at morn;

Scott: *Lay of the Last Minstrel*
Edinburgh: Ballantyne, 1806
$4\frac{1}{4}'' \times 2\frac{1}{4}''$

# DAVISON'S
# 𝕻𝖔𝖊𝖙𝖎𝖈𝖆𝖑 𝕽𝖍𝖆𝖕𝖘𝖔𝖉𝖞.

WITH

## A PREFACE,

BY

## SIR EGERTON BRYDGES, K.J.

"Never durst Poet touch a pen to write,
Until his ink were temper'd with Love's sighs;
And then his lines would ravish savage ears,
And plant in Tyrants mild humanity."   *Shakesp.*

KENT.

𝕻𝖗𝖎𝖓𝖙𝖊𝖉 𝖆𝖙 𝖙𝖍𝖊 𝖕𝖗𝖎𝖇𝖆𝖙𝖊 𝕻𝖗𝖊𝖘𝖘 𝖔𝖋 𝕷𝖊𝖊 𝕻𝖗𝖎𝖔𝖗𝖞;

BY JOHNSON AND WARWICK.

1814.

Davison: *Poetical Rhapsody*
Lee Priory: Johnson and Warwick, 1814
$6\frac{7}{8}'' \times 3\frac{3}{4}''$

## ADVERTISEMENT

TO

### *THE FIRST PORTION OF THIS EDITION.*

HE Collection of Elizabethan Poetry, which is now again introduced to the curious through the LEE PRIORY Press, has long been a desideratum among the lovers of our old English literature: for, though it passed through four editions in the reign of King James I. (1602, 1608, 1611, 1621,) it has for at least a century been so rare, that very few have had an opportunity of being gratified with the perusal of it.

The intrinsic merit of the pieces, which it contains, is intended to form the subject of an Introduction, which is kept back till the printers have had time to complete the impression of the original work.

FRANCIS DAVISON, the collector, and in part author, of these poems, was the son of

Davison: *Poetical Rhapsody*
Lee Priory: Johnson and Warwick, 1814
$6\frac{7}{8}'' \times 3\frac{3}{4}''$

THE

# FABLES OF ÆSOP,

AND OTHERS,

WITH DESIGNS ON WOOD,

BY

THOMAS BEWICK

*The wisest of the Ancients delivered their Conceptions of the Deity, and their Lessons of Morality, in Fables and Parables."*

NEWCASTLE:

PRINTED BY E. WALKER, FOR T. BEWICK AND SON.
SOLD BY THEM, LONGMAN AND CO. LONDON,
AND ALL BOOKSELLERS.

1818.

Aesop: *Fables*

Newcastle: Walker and Bewick, 1818

$6\frac{1}{8}'' \times 3\frac{1}{4}''$

## THE ORIGINAL PREFACE.

To those who attentively consider the subject of Natural History, as displayed in the animal creation, it will appear, that though much has been done to explore the intricate paths of Nature, and follow her through all her various windings, much yet remains to be done before the great œconomy is completely developed. Notwithstanding the laborious and not unsuccessful inquiries of ingenious men in all ages, the subject is far from being exhausted. Systems have been formed and exploded, and new ones have appeared in their stead; but, like skeletons injudiciously put together, they give but an imperfect idea of that order and symmetry to which they are intended to be subservient: they have, however, their use, but it is chiefly the skilful practitioner who is enabled to profit by them; to the less informed they appear obscure and perplexing, and too frequently deter him from the great object of his pursuit.

To investigate, with any tolerable degree of success, the more retired and distant parts of the animal œconomy, is a task of no small difficulty. An enquiry so desirable and so eminently useful would require the united efforts of many to give it the desired success. Men of leisure, of all descriptions, residing in the country, could scarcely find a more delightful employment than in attempting to elucidate, from their own observations, the various branches of Natural

VOL. I. b

Aesop: *Fables*

Newcastle: Walker and Bewick, 1818

$6\frac{1}{4}'' \times 3\frac{1}{4}''$

# Q. HORATII FLACCI OPERA
## RECENSUIT ET ILLUSTRAVIT
## FREDERICUS G. DOERING
### ACCEDUNT INDICES
### LOCUPLETISSIMI.

EDITIO NOVA, AUCTIOR ET EMENDATIOR.

M DCCC XXXVIII.

**OXONII: D. A. TALBOYS.**

LONDINI: WHITTAKER ET CO.;
LONGMAN, ORME, BROWN, GREEN, ET LONGMANS;
ET T. TEGG ET FILIUS.

Horatius: *Opera*
Oxford: D. A. Talboys, 1838
$6\frac{7}{8}'' \times 3\frac{5}{8}''$

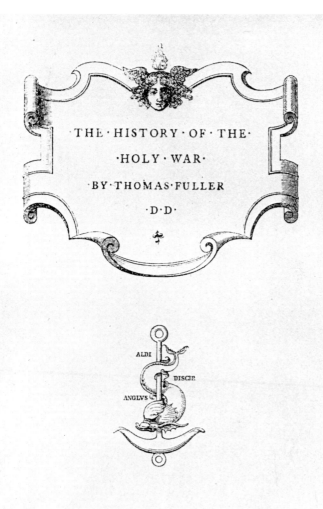

THE·HISTORY·OF·THE·
·HOLY·WAR·
·BY·THOMAS·FULLER
·D·D·

ALDI

DISCIP.

ANGLVS

LONDON
WILLIAM PICKERING
1840

Fuller: *History of the Holy War*
London: Pickering and Whittingham, 1840
$5\frac{1}{2}'' \times 3''$

TO HIS WORTHY AND LEARNED FRIEND,

## MR. THOMAS FULLER,

UPON HIS EXCELLENTLY COMPOSED HISTORY OF THE

HOLY WAR.

CAPTAIN of arts, in this thy Holy War
My muse desires to be thy trumpeter,
In thy just praise to spend a blast or two,
For this is all that she (poor thing) can do.

Peter the Hermit, like an angry owl,
Would needs go fight all armed in his cowl.
What, had the holy man nought else to do,
But thus to lose his blood and credit too?
Seeking to win Christ's sepulchre, God wot,
He found his own; this was the ground he got.
Except he got more ground, when he one day
Besieging Antioch fiercely ran away.
Much wiser was the Pope: at home he stayed,
And made the world believe he wept and prayed.
Meanwhile (behold the fruit of feigned tears)
He sets the world together by the ears.
His head serves him, whilst others use their hands:
Whilst princes lose their lives, he gets their lands.
To win the Holy Land what need kings roam?
The pope can make a Holy Land at home
By making it his own: then for a fashion,
'Tis said to come by Constantine's donation.
For all this fox-craft, I have leave (I hope)
To think my friend far wiser than the pope
And hermit both: he deals in holy wars,
Not as a stickler in those fruitless jars,
But a composer rather: hence this book;
Whereon whilst I with greedy eyes do look,
Methinks I travel through the Holy Land,
Viewing the sacred objects on each hand.
Here mounts (methinks), like Olivet, brave sense;
There flows a Jordan of pure eloquence:
A temple rich in ornament I find
Presented here to my admiring mind.
Strange force of Art! the ruined holy city
Breeds admiration in me now, not pity.
To testify her liking, here my muse
Makes solemn vows, as holy pilgrims use.

Fuller: *History of the Holy War*

London: Pickering and Whittingham, 1840

$5\frac{3}{8}'' \times 2\frac{1}{2}''$

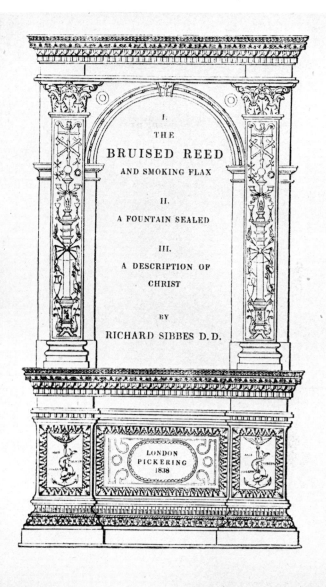

Sibbes: *The Bruised Reed*

London: Pickering and Whittingham, 1838

$5\frac{1}{2}'' \times 3\frac{1}{8}''$

## TO THE RIGHT HONOURABLE
# THE LADY DALKEITH,
### LADY GOVERNESS TO HER HIGHNESS
### THE PRINCESS HENRIETTA.

MADAM,

*IT is unsafe in these dangerous days for any to go abroad without a convoy, or, at the least, a pass; my book hath both in being dedicated to your honour. The apostle saith, Who planteth a vineyard, and eateth not of the fruit thereof?* \* *I am one of your honour's planting, and could heartily wish, that the fruit I bring forth were worthy to be tasted by your judicious palate. Howsoever, accept these grapes, if not for their goodness, for their novelty : though not sweetest relished, they are soonest ripe, being the first fruits of Exeter press, presented unto you. And if ever my ingratitude should forget my obligations to your honour, these black lines will turn red, and blush his unworthiness that wrote them. In*

\* 1 Cor. ix. 7.

B

Sibbes: *The Bruised Reed*

London: Pickering and Whittingham, 1838

$5\frac{1}{4}'' \times 2\frac{5}{8}''$

## GOOD THOUGHTS

IN BAD TIMES, GOOD THOUGHTS IN WORSE
TIMES, MIXT CONTEMPLATIONS
IN BETTER TIMES,

BY THOMAS FULLER D. D.

TO WHICH IS ADDED

THE CAUSE AND CURE OF A WOUNDED
CONSCIENCE

LONDON
WILLIAM PICKERING
MDCCCXLI

Fuller: *Good Thoughts*
London: Pickering and Whittingham, 1841
$5\frac{1}{2}'' \times 2\frac{1}{2}''$

# The Passion of our Lord Jesus Christ,

## *pourtrayed by Albert Durer.*

### EDITED BY HENRY COLE,

AN ASSISTANT KEEPER OF THE
PUBLIC RECORDS.

ॐ

## London:

Joſeph Cundall, 12, Old Bond Street; William Pickering,
177, Piccadilly; George Bell, 186, Fleet Street;
J. H. Parker, Oxford; J. and J. J.
Deighton, Cambridge.

1844.

Cole: *The Passion of Our Lord*
London: Pickering and Whittingham, 1844
$5\frac{1}{8}'' \times 3\frac{3}{4}''$

# Hortus Animae
OR
## GARDEN OF THE SOUL.

### CHRISTIAN DOCTRINE,
Or, a Summary of Chriftian Faith and Morality.

#### SECT. I.

What every Chriftian muft believe.

*Without Faith it is impoffible to pleafe God.* Heb. xi. 6.

VERY Chriftian muft believe that there is one God, and no more than one God ; that this God is a pure Spirit, the Lord and Maker of heaven and earth, who has neither beginning nor end ; but is always the fame ; is everywhere prefent; knows and fees all things, can do all things, whatfoever He pleafes, and is infinite in all perfections.

2. Every Chriftian is bound to believe that in this *one* God there are three feveral Perfons, perfectly equal, and of the fame fubftance ; the Father, who proceeds from no one : the Son, who is born of the Father before all ages ; and the Holy Ghoft, who proceeds eternally from the Father and the Son ; and that thefe perfons have all the fame age, the fame power, and the fame wifdom, and are all three one and the fame Lord, one and the fame God.

*Hortus Animae*

London: John Philip, 1860

$4\frac{7}{8}'' \times 3''$

# RELIQUES OF OLD LONDON UPON THE BANKS OF THE THAMES & IN THE SUBURBS SOUTH OF THE RIVER

DRAWN IN LITHOGRAPHY BY

## T. R. WAY

WITH AN INTRODUCTION AND DESCRIPTIONS BY

## H. B. WHEATLEY, F.S.A.

LONDON: GEORGE BELL AND SONS: MDCCCXCIX

Way: *Reliques of Old London*
London: Chiswick Press, 1899
$8'' \times 6\frac{1}{4}''$

Afloat
again

# CHAPTER XXIV. UP THE THAMES: THE SECOND DAY.

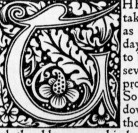

HEY were not slow to take my hint; & indeed, as to the mere time of day, it was best for us to be off, as it was past seven o'clock, & the day promised to be very hot. So we got up and went down to our boat; Ellen thoughtful and abstracted; the old man very kind and courteous, as if to make up for his crabbedness of opinion. Clara was cheerful & natural, but a little subdued, I thought; and she at least was not sorry to be gone, and often looked shyly and timidly at Ellen and her strange wild beauty. So we got into the boat, Dick saying as he took his place, "Well, it is a fine day!" and the old man answering "What! you like that, do you?" once more; and presently Dick was sending the bows swiftly through the slow weed-checked stream. I turned round as we got into mid-stream, and waving my hand to our hosts, saw Ellen leaning on the old man's shoulder, and caressing his healthy apple-red cheek, and quite a keen pang smote me as I thought how I should never see the beautiful girl again. Presently I insisted on taking the sculls, and I rowed a good deal that day; which no doubt accounts for the fact that we got very late

230

Morris: *News from Nowhere*

Kelmscott Press, 1892

$5\frac{5}{8}'' \times 4\frac{1}{4}''$

U

to the place which **Dick** had aimed at. **Clara was Once a**
particularly affectionate to **Dick**, as I noticed from **school**
the rowing thwart; but as for him, he was as frank-
ly kind and merry as ever; and I was glad to see it,
as a man of his temperament could not have taken
her caresses cheerfully and without embarrass-
ment if he had been at all entangled by the fairy
of our last night's abode.

NEED say little about the lovely reaches of the river here. I duly no-ted that absence of cockney villas which the old man had lamented; and I saw with pleasure that my old enemies the "Gothic" cast-iron bridges had been replaced by handsome oak and stone ones. Also the banks of the forest that we passed through had lost their courtly game-keep-erish trimness, and were as wild and beautiful as need be, though the trees were clearly well seen to. I thought it best, in order to get the most direct information, to play the innocent about **Eton &** **Windsor**; but **Dick** volunteered his knowledge to me as we lay in **Datchet** lock about the first. Quoth he: ❡ "Up yonder are some beautiful old buildings, which were built for a great college or teaching-place by one of the mediæval kings... Edward the Sixth, I think" (I smiled to myself at his rather natural blunder). "He meant poor peo-ple's sons to be taught there what knowledge was going in his days; but it was a matter of course that

231

Morris: *News from Nowhere*

Kelmscott Press, 1892

$5\frac{5}{8}'' \times 4\frac{1}{8}''$

# IN THE BEGINNING

GOD CREATED THE HEAVEN AND THE EARTH. ⸿ AND
THE EARTH WAS WITHOUT FORM, AND VOID; AND
DARKNESS WAS UPON THE FACE OF THE DEEP, & THE
SPIRIT OF GOD MOVED UPON THE FACE OF THE WATERS.
⸿ And God said, Let there be light: & there was light. And God saw the light,
that it was good: & God divided the light from the darkness. And God called
the light Day, and the darkness he called Night. And the evening and the
morning were the first day. ⸿ And God said, Let there be a firmament in the
midst of the waters, & let it divide the waters from the waters. And God made
the firmament, and divided the waters which were under the firmament from
the waters which were above the firmament: & it was so. And God called the
firmament Heaven. And the evening & the morning were the second day.
⸿ And God said, Let the waters under the heaven be gathered together unto
one place, and let the dry land appear: and it was so. And God called the dry
land Earth; and the gathering together of the waters called he Seas: and God
saw that it was good. And God said, Let the earth bring forth grass, the herb
yielding seed, and the fruit tree yielding fruit after his kind, whose seed is in
itself, upon the earth: & it was so. And the earth brought forth grass, & herb
yielding seed after his kind, & the tree yielding fruit, whose seed was in itself,
after his kind: and God saw that it was good. And the evening & the morning
were the third day. ⸿ And God said, Let there be lights in the firmament of
the heaven to divide the day from the night: and let them be for signs, and for
seasons, and for days, & years: and let them be for lights in the firmament of
the heaven to give light upon the earth: & it was so. And God made two great
lights; the greater light to rule the day, and the lesser light to rule the night: he
made the stars also. And God set them in the firmament of the heaven to give
light upon the earth, and to rule over the day and over the night, & to divide
the light from the darkness: and God saw that it was good. And the evening
and the morning were the fourth day. ⸿ And God said, Let the waters bring
forth abundantly the moving creature that hath life, and fowl that may fly
above the earth in the open firmament of heaven. And God created great
whales, & every living creature that moveth, which the waters brought forth
abundantly, after their kind, & every winged fowl after his kind: & God saw
that it was good. And God blessed them, saying, Be fruitful, & multiply, and
fill the waters in the seas, and let fowl multiply in the earth. And the evening
& the morning were the fifth day. ⸿ And God said, Let the earth bring forth
the living creature after his kind, cattle, and creeping thing, and beast of the
earth after his kind: and it was so. And God made the beast of the earth after
his kind, and cattle after their kind, and every thing that creepeth upon the

27

*The Holy Bible*

London: The Doves Press, 1903–5

$9\frac{1}{8}'' \times 6\frac{3}{8}''$

# A HISTORY OF THE HOLY EUCHARIST IN GREAT BRITAIN

*BY T. E. BRIDGETT, C.SS.R.*
*With Notes by H. THURSTON, S.J.*

LONDON
**BURNS & OATES**
ORCHARD STREET
M CM VIII

Bridgett and Thurston: *History of the Holy Eucharist*

London: Arden Press, 1908

$9\frac{7}{8}'' \times 5\frac{1}{2}''$

THE ORDER FOR

# MORNING PRAYER,

### DAILY THROUGHOUT THE YEAR.

¶ At the beginning of Morning Prayer the Minister shall read with a loud voice some one or more of these Sentences of the Scriptures that follow. And then he shall say that which is written after the said Sentences.

Ezekiel xviii. 27.

HEN the wicked man turneth away from his wickedness that he hath committed, and doeth that which is lawful and right, he shall save his soul alive.

Psalm li. 3. I acknowledge my transgressions, and my sin is ever before me.

Psalm li. 9. Hide thy face from my sins, and blot out all mine iniquities.

Psalm li. 17. The sacrifices of God are a broken spirit: a broken and a contrite heart, O God, thou wilt not despise.

Joel ii. 13. Rend your heart, and not your garments, and turn unto the Lord your God: for he is gracious and merciful, slow to anger, and of great kindness, and repenteth him of the evil.

Dan. ix. 9, 10. To the Lord our God belong mercies and forgivenesses, though we have rebelled against him: neither have we obeyed the voice of the Lord our God, to walk in his laws which he set before us.

O Lord, correct me, but with judgement; not in thine anger, lest thou bring me to nothing. Jer. x. 24. Psalm vi. 1.

Repent ye; for the Kingdom of heaven is at hand. St. Matt. iii. 2.

I will arise, and go to my father, and will say unto him, Father, I have sinned against heaven, and before thee, and am no more worthy to be called thy son. St. Luke xv. 18, 19.

Enter not into judgement with thy servant, O Lord; for in thy sight shall no man living be justified. Psalm cxliii. 2.

If we say that we have no sin, we deceive ourselves, and the truth is not in us: but, if we confess our sins, he is faithful and just to forgive us our sins, and to cleanse us from all unrighteousness. St. John i. 8, 9.

A                    DEARLY

Book of Common Prayer

Oxford University Press, 1911

$9\frac{3}{4}'' \times 7\frac{7}{8}''$

# THE ORDER OF

the Administration of

## THE LORD'S SUPPER

### OR

## HOLY COMMUNION

Together with the Orders of

CONFIRMATION

THE SOLEMNIZATION OF MATRIMONY

AND THE CHURCHING OF WOMEN

According to the Use of

## THE CHURCH OF ENGLAND

*Cum*          *Privilegio*

### OXFORD

### AT THE UNIVERSITY PRESS

MCMXI

*Book of Common Prayer*

Oxford University Press, 1911

$11\frac{1}{2}'' \times 7\frac{5}{8}''$

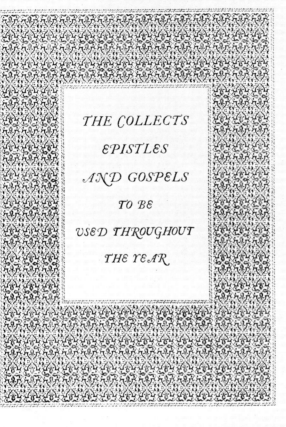

THE COLLECTS
EPISTLES
AND GOSPELS
TO BE
USED THROUGHOUT
THE YEAR

Book of Common Prayer
Oxford University Press, 1911
$10\frac{3}{8}'' \times 7\frac{1}{2}''$

# BODLEIAN LIBRARY
# SHAKESPEARE EXHIBITION
## 1916

### CLASS A.   EARLY WORKS

1   VENUS AND ADONIS, 1593.
The only copy of the first edition of
Shakespeare's first publication.

Venus and Adonis.  [*motto, then device*]
 London Imprinted by Richard Field, and are to
 be sold at the signe of the white Greyhound
 in Paules Church-yard.  1593.  4°: signn.
 A¹ B–G⁴ H².

Unique copy, reproduced in facsimile by Ashbee in 1867, by
Griggs in 1886, and by Lee in 1905.  The motto on the title-
page is from Ovid (*Amores* I. xv. 35–6):
   ' Vilia miretur vulgus : mihi flavus Apollo
    Pocula Castalia plena ministret aqua ',
which Marlowe translated
   ' Let base-conceited wits admire vile things,
   Fair Phœbus lead me to the Muses' springs ! '
This and *Lucrece* were the only two works published with the
author's sanction and co-operation.  The preface declares the

B

*Catalogue of the Shakespeare Exhibition*
Oxford University Press, 1916
$6\frac{1}{4}'' \times 3\frac{7}{8}''$

# D<sup>r</sup> John RADCLIFFE

## A SKETCH

## *OF HIS LIFE*

### WITH AN ACCOUNT

### OF HIS

# FELLOWS

### AND

# FOUNDATIONS

By *J. B. Nias,* M.D., M.R.C.P.

*Radcliffe Travelling Fellow* 1882–5

# *O X F O R D*

At the CLARENDON PRESS *A.D.* 1918

Nias: *Dr. John Radcliffe*

Oxford University Press, 1918

$6\frac{5}{8}'' \times 3\frac{3}{4}''$

# SHAKESPEARE'S
# Use of Song
## With the Text of
# The Principal Songs

by

### Richmond Noble, M.A.
Lincoln College, Oxford

## OXFORD UNIVERSITY PRESS
## HUMPHREY MILFORD
### M CM XXIII

Noble: *Shakespeare's Use of Song*
Oxford University Press, 1923
$7\frac{1}{4}'' \times 4\frac{1}{8}''$

# THE
# AUTHORISED VERSION

## OF THE

# ENGLISH BIBLE
## 1611

EDITED BY

## WILLIAM ALDIS WRIGHT, M.A.

VICE-MASTER OF TRINITY COLLEGE, CAMBRIDGE

### VOLUME I

### Cambridge
### at the University Press
### 1909

*The English Bible*
Cambridge University Press, 1909
$6\frac{1}{8}'' \times 3\frac{5}{8}''$

## ADDRESS AT THE UNVEILING OF THE ROLL OF HONOUR OF THE CAMBRIDGE TIPPERARY CLUB. BY THE PROVOST OF KING'S COLLEGE.

TODAY a great record is brought before us. The Roll of Honour of this Club is unveiled. Each name that is written upon it brings to some one of you who hear me a memory which I think must be more precious than, any gift that could be given to you, except the gift of one more sight of the kinsman or the friend. But not to you alone are these memories precious. We also, even if we did not know them, are proud of our fellow citizens; nay, there is not a man, woman, or child in the land who does not now,—who for many a year to come will not,—honour the men and boys who went forth, not knowing whither they went, and gave for England all that they had to give.

Four or five years ago, what did each one of these think would be the course of his life? Most, I suppose, thought of years spent in some honest work or trade, of a wife, home, and children, a quiet old age, and a grave among those he had known. Even to those who had planned something more adventurous, a life over seas, or the career of a sailor or a soldier, it did not seem the most likely thing that they would die a death of violence.

There came a day which changed all that: a day when it

1

*Address at the Tipperary Club*

Cambridge University Press, 1918

$7'' \times 4\frac{1}{8}''$

Juliet; Venice for Shylock and for Othello as handily as for Gratiano; and Launce and Launcelot Gobbo are brothers and might inhabit either. In the original version of that most English of comedies, *Every Man in his Humour*, Jonson laid the scene in Florence and gave his characters Italian names. Few will deny that by transferring the scene to London and turning his eccentrics into English men and women he made—by this process alone—a vastly better play; that in his native-grown Comedy of Humours this increase of realism increases his vivacity and verisimilitude. The audience approved, and the successors and congeners of *Every Man in his Humour*—*Epicoene*, *The Alchemist*, *Bartholomew's Fair*—were duly located in or near London.

> Our *Scene* is *London*, 'cause we would make knowne
> No countries mirth is better then our owne...
> (Prologue to *The Alchemist*, 1610.)

The apology, however, hints the innovation. In 1598 Jonson would stage his British comedy in Florence as unhesitatingly as, ten years or so later, Webster staged his Italianate *White Devil* in Rome or Padua; or—shall we say?—with no more trouble of artistic conscience than Shakespeare felt in dodging the centuries and dragging the right Renaissance scoundrel Iachimo into a supposed early-British *Tragedie of Cymbeline*. 'Somewhere in Italy' was in fact the spot where an Elizabethan playwright and his audience started upon agreed terms. Apart from the tradition and the romance of it, this convention of Italy conveniently accommodated the players, under a wide range of magnificent titles, with a still wider wardrobe of magnificent and miscellaneous costumes.

Guess-work suggests that in *The Two Gentlemen of Verona* Shakespeare recast an old lost play *The History of Felix and Philiomena*, entered in the Revels Accounts, 1584–5, as having been acted by the Queen's company at Greenwich 'on the sondaie next after neweyeares daie at

Shakespeare: *Two Gentlemen of Verona*

Cambridge University Press, 1921

$5\frac{1}{4}'' \times 2\frac{7}{8}''$

Higginson: *Fifteen Sonnets of Petrarch*

Cambridge, U.S.A.: Bruce Rogers, Riverside Press, 1903

$6\frac{1}{2}'' \times 3\frac{3}{4}''$

INTRODUCTION

*a doubtful blessing to the human race, that the in-*
*stinct of translation still prevails, stronger than rea-*
*son ; and after one has once yielded to it, then each*
*untranslated favorite is like the trees round a back-*
*woodsman's clearing, each of which stands, a silent*
*defiance, until he has cut it down. Let us try the axe*
*again. This is to Laura singing (*Quando Amor*).*

*As I look across the bay, there is seen resting over*
*all the hills, and even upon every distant sail, an*
*enchanted veil of palest blue, that seems woven out*
*of the very souls of happy days,— a bridal veil,*
*with which the sunshine weds this soft landscape in*
*summer. Such and so indescribable is the atmos-*
*pheric film that hangs over these poems of* Petrarch's*;*
*there is a delicate haze about the words, that van-*
*ishes when you touch them, and reappears as you re-*
*cede. How it clings, for instance, round this sonnet*
*(*Aura che quelle chiome*) !*

*Consider also the pure and reverential tenderness*
*of one like this (*Qual donna attende*). A compan-*
*ion sonnet, on the other hand (*O passi sparsi*),*
*seems rather to be of the Shakespearean type ; the*
*successive phrases set sail, one by one, like a yacht*
*squadron ; each spreads its graceful wings and glides*

ix

Higginson: *Fifteen Sonnets of Petrarch*

Cambridge, U.S.A.: Bruce Rogers, Riverside Press, 1903

$4\frac{1}{2}'' \times 2\frac{3}{4}''$

GEORGICS

*OF VIRGIL*

*TRANSLATED FROM THE*

*LATIN INTO ENGLISH BY*

*J. W. MACKAIL FELLOW OF*

*BALLIOL COLLEGE OXFORD*

*Non illum nostri possunt*

*mutare labores*

B    R

The Riverside Press

Mackail: *Georgics of Virgil*

Cambridge, U.S.A.: Bruce Rogers, Riverside Press, 1904

$7\frac{1}{4}'' \times 4\frac{3}{8}''$

Walton: *Compleat Angler*

Cambridge, U.S.A.: Bruce Rogers, Riverside Press, 1909

$5\frac{1}{4}'' \times 3\frac{1}{8}''$

X

TO THE

*Reader of this Discourse*

BUT ESPECIALLY TO

THE HONEST

ANGLER

I Think fit to tell thee these following truths; that I did not undertake to write, or to publish this Discourse of Fish and Fishing, to please my self, and that I wish it may not displease others; for I have confest there are many defects in it. And yet, I can not doubt, but that by it, some readers may receive so much profit or pleasure, as if they be not very busie men, may make it not un-

Walton: *Compleat Angler*

Cambridge, U.S.A.: Bruce Rogers, Riverside Press, 1909

$4\frac{1}{8}'' \times 2\frac{1}{8}''$

# LXXV SONNETS

BY

*William Wordsworth*

*Houghton Mifflin Company*
*Boston & New York*

Wordsworth: *Seventy-five Sonnets*
Cambridge, U.S.A.: Bruce Rogers, Riverside Press, 1910
$4\frac{3}{4}'' \times 2\frac{1}{4}''$

# M<sup>R</sup> WALPOLE'S FRIENDS
## IN BOSTON

❧

**M**ANY promiſing enter-
priſes have been organized
into an early death. On
the rocks of the elaborate plan and the
ſhoals of the careful ſyſtem are the
wrecks of many good ſhips. The Walpole Society find the ſafeſt anchorage

Dana: *Mr. Walpole's Friends in Boston*
Cambridge, U.S.A.: Bruce Rogers, Riverside Press, 1911
$5\frac{7}{8}'' \times 3''$

# INTRODUCTION

*To the Edition of* 1825.

## By THEODORE DWIGHT.

THIS *is not a work of fiction, as the scarcity of old American manuscripts may induce some to imagine; but it is a faithful copy from a diary in the author's own hand-writing, compiled soon after her return home, as it appears, from notes recorded daily, while on the road. She was a resident of Boston, and a lady of uncommon literary attainments, as well as of great taste and strength of mind. She was called Madam Knight, out of respect to her character,*

*The Journal of Madam Knight*
Bruce Rogers, at the Press of W. E. Rudge, 1920
$5\frac{1}{4}'' \times 2\frac{5}{8}''$

# THE

# JOURNAL

## OF

# Madam *KNIGHT*.

❖❖❖❖❖❖❖❖❖❖❖❖❖❖❖❖❖❖

*Monday, Octb'r. yᵉ second,*
*1704.*

ABOUT three o'clock afternoon, I
begun my Journey from Boſton
to New-Haven; being about two Hundred Mile. My Kinsman, Capt. Robertꜰ
Luiſt, waited on me as farr as Dedham,
where I was to meet yᵉ Weſtern poſt.

I

*The Journal of Madam Knight*
Bruce Rogers, at the Press of W. E. Rudge, 1920
$5\frac{1}{4}'' \times 2\frac{5}{8}''$

Hudson: *Ralph Herne*

Bruce Rogers, at the Press of W. E. Rudge, 1923

$6\frac{5}{8}'' \times 4\frac{1}{4}''$

# The Felicities of Sixty

## By ISAAC H. LIONBERGER

### BOSTON
#### The Club of Odd Volumes
#### 1922

Lionberger: *The Felicities of Sixty*
Boston, U.S.A.: D. B. Updike, Merrymount Press, 1922
$5'' \times 3\frac{1}{8}''$

# THE FELICITIES OF SIXTY

I N MY Sixtieth Year, a wise woman of more than eighty said to me: "I congratulate you: you have begun to live after sixty years of preparation, and are now wise enough to govern yourself and help others. The best part of life is between sixty and eighty."

I pondered her saying, testing its truth by my own experience. I think she was right. I think so because my opinion of friends and enemies, of life and the meaning of life, has undergone a marked and significant change in which I find a distinct and abiding happiness. We have, at

Lionberger: *The Felicities of Sixty*

Boston, U.S.A.: D. B. Updike, Merrymount Press, 1922

$4\frac{7}{8}'' \times 3''$

# Charles Lamb

A LETTER regarding Roast Pig to WILLIAM HAZLITT
and
A LETTER on Friendship to ROBERT LLOYD
together with
A DISSERTATION on ROAST PIG

Privately Printed for his Friends by
W. K. BIXBY
1922

Lamb: *Dissertation concerning roast pig*
Boston, U.S.A.: D. B. Updike, Merrymount Press, 1922
$5\frac{1}{4}'' \times 3\frac{7}{8}''$

## Mrs. Amory's Letters

———

I

Havre, Nov' 1st, 1833.

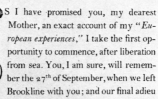

A S I have promised you, my dearest Mother, an exact account of my *European experiences,"* I take the first opportunity to commence, after liberation from sea. You, I am sure, will remember the 27th of September, when we left Brookline with you; and our final adieu at Dedham; that parting scene I shall long remember—such moments are not easily obliterated from the memory! We reached Providence to sleep, after a melancholy ride, which, however, was much enlivened to Mr Amory by Mr E. Preble's company, who very kindly attended us to N. York, and remained there with us till the eve before we sailed. Before leaving Providence we paid a long visit to our friends the Arnolds, who received us with even more than their usual kindnefs. At noon we took pafsage in the Steamboat, where among others of our acquaintance, we recognized Mr & Mrs N. Amory, who, however, stopped at Newport. In spite of my

*The Wedding Journey of Charles and Martha Amory*
Boston, U.S.A.: D. B. Updike, Merrymount Press, 1922
$5\frac{3}{4}'' \times 4\frac{1}{2}''$

THE JOURNAL OF

*MRS. JOHN AMORY*

1775

EFT Boston Wenesday 24 May 1775, about 9' oClock
in the forenoon—in a Schooner, bound to Marblehead,
where we arriv'd about four o'Clock the same day, &
went first on board the *Minerva*,— Brother & Sister
Payne & M' Eliot were there waiting for us — we then went on
shore at Marblehead, drank Tea with M' & M" Eliot at their lodg-
ings, sup'd & lodg'd at the Inn with Brother Payne — M" Jackson
with us—

*Thursday* 25ᵗ dined at the Inn, then went with Brother & Sister
Payne to Salem, & lodg'd at M' Mascarene's—

*Fryday* 26 —After Breakfast, return'd to Marblehead, Brother &
Sister Payne with us, & dined with M' Eliot—after dinner went on
board the *Minerva*, & soon had the pleasure of seeing M' & M"
Greene coming into the harbour.— we waited to welcome them
on board, then went on shore to drink Tea, & then took leave of
our friends & return'd on board late in the Evening—

*Saturday May* 27. 1775 — About 9' oClock in the forenoon, sat sail
from Marblehead in the Ship *Minerva* Capt. John Calahan for

[ 3 ]

*Journal of Mrs. John Amory*

Boston, U.S.A.: D. B. Updike, Merrymount Press, 1923

7" × 5"

# HET EIGEN RIJK

DOOR

ALBERT VERWEY

DE ZILVERDISTEL
'S GRAVENHAGE, MDCCCCXII

Verwey: *Het Eigen Rijk*

Enschedé en Zonen for the Zilverdistel Press, 1912

$5\frac{3}{8}'' \times 4\frac{1}{4}''$

### LANSELOET

Lanſeloet van
Denemerken

AY GOD HERE hoe mach dit ſijn
Dat ic die ſcone ſanderijn
Aldus met herten hebbe beſeten
Nochtan wert mi verweten
Van mijnder moeder alle daghe
Dat ic mine minne ſoe neder draghe
Dies horic menich ſpitich woort
Maer haer minne heeft mi ſoe doerboert
Dat icſe ghelaten niet en can
Ic en moet haer altoes ſpreken an
Als icſe metten oghen aneſcouwe
Dies heeft mijn moeder groten rouwe
Daer omme ſoe moet verborghen ſijn.
Nv willic hier wachten die vrouwe mijn
Onder deſen neghelentier
Want ſi ſal hier comen ſcier
Dat wetic wel in deſen bogaert.

### SANDERIJN

❦O edel ridder van hogher aert,
God die alle dinc vermach
Die moet v gheuen goeden dach
Edel ridder van herten vri.

### LANSELOET

O ſcone maghet, god die ſi ons bi
Ende moet v ende mi in doghden ſparen

7

*Lanseloet Van Denemerken*

Enschedé en Zonen for the Zilverdistel Press, 1913

$5'' \times 3\frac{3}{8}''$

# SCHILLER
## DRAMATISCHE
## DICHTUNGEN
## BAND I

## MCMV
## LEIPZIG
## IM INSELVERLAG

Schiller: *Dramatische Dichtungen*

Carl Ernest Poeschel for the Insel-Verlag, 1905

$5\frac{5}{8}'' \times 3\frac{1}{8}''$

A Minos mi portò; e quegli attorse
　　otto volte la coda al dosso duro;
　　e, poi che per gran rabbia la si morse,
Disse: ‹ Questi è de' rei del fuoco furo ›;
　　per ch' io là dove vedi son perduto,
　　e sì vestito andando mi rancuro. »
Quand' egli ebbe il suo dir così compiuto,
　　la fiamma dolorando si partio,
　　torcendo e dibattendo il corno acuto.
Noi passammo oltre, ed io e il duca mio,
　　su per lo scoglio infino in su l'altr' arco
　　che copre il fosso in che si paga il fio
A quei che scommettendo acquistan carco.


Canto ventesimottavo.

CHI PORIA MAI PUR CON
　　parole sciolte / dicer del sangue
　　e delle piaghe appieno, / ch' i'
　　ora vidi, per narrar più volte?
Ogni lingua per certo verria meno
　　per lo nostro sermone e per la mente,
　　c' hanno a tanto comprender poco seno.
S' ei s' adunasse ancor tutta la gente,
　　che già in su la fortunata terra
　　di Puglia fu del suo sangue dolente
Per li Troiani, e per la lunga guerra
　　che dell' anella fe' sì alte spoglie,
　　come Livio scrive, che non erra;
Con quella che sentì di colpi doglie
　　per contrastare a Roberto Guiscardo,
　　e l' altra, il cui ossame ancor s' accoglie
122

Dante: *Divina Commedia*

Munich: Bremer Presse, 1924

$8\frac{3}{4}'' \times 3\frac{5}{8}''$

# INDEX OF PRINTERS
# AND CRAFTSMEN

# INDEX OF PRINTERS
# AND CRAFTSMEN

*(Numbers in italics refer to references in the text; otherwise the references are to plates)*